THE WAR
AGAINST THE
TERRORISTS

THE WAR

THE

AGAINST TERRORISTS

How to Win It

Gayle Rivers

STEIN AND DAY/Publishers/New York

First published in 1986
Copyright © 1986 by Littopus S. A. and
   The Colophon Corporation
All rights reserved, Stein and Day, Incorporated
Designed by Louis A. Ditizio
Printed in the United States of America

STEIN AND DAY/*Publishers*
Scarborough House
Briarcliff Manor, N.Y. 10510

Library of Congress Cataloging-in-Publication Data

Rivers, Gayle.
   The war against the terrorists.

   1. Terrorism. 2. Terrorism—Prevention. I. Title.
HV6431.R58 1986   363.3′2   85-40961
ISBN 0-8128-3093-8

This book is dedicated
to the men and women who daily fight
the war against the terrorists
and in particular to the men of the bomb disposal squads
who when all else has failed
go in alone.

January 15, 1986

"I declare that we shall train them for terrorist and suicide missions and allocate trainers for them and place all the weapons needed for such missions at their disposal."

—Muammar el-Qaddafi,
Tripoli, January 15, 1986
quoted in *The New York Times*

"One quarter of the nations of the world are at war."

—Caspar Weinberger,
U.S. Secretary of Defense
January 15, 1986

"The Western democracies are still not aware of it as warfare against them."

—Lord Chalfont
January 15, 1986

"The one means that wins
the easiest victory over
reason: terror and force."

—Adolf Hitler,
Mein Kampf

Contents

THE WAR
AGAINST THE
TERRORISTS

1

The Man behind
the Terrorist Mask

If one is about to clean house, a good first step is to get rid of the garbage. But one man's garbage is another man's keepsake. Garbage is what a person wants to get rid of. What I want to get rid of is the human garbage that willfully perpetrates outrages against the rest of humanity and whom we have come to call terrorists.

A victim who has looked a terrorist in the eyes often learns more in those few seconds than other people can by reading about terrorism in newspapers for years. Leon Klinghoffer, the 69-year-old American invalid in his wheelchair, knew what the terrorist is really like in those seconds before he was shot in the chest and face and thrown overboard from the *Achille Lauro,* his wheelchair flung into the sea after him. If, as it was reported by a witness, he bit one of the terrorists just before being shot, he certainly knew.

Judge Stanley Kubacki of Philadelphia, a passenger on the *Achille Lauro,* reported that the hijackers forced his wife, Sophia, and two other women to hold hand grenades with the pins removed. Other hostages were forced to sit

15

close to the women and watch. "If one of these women fell asleep or fainted," the judge said, "we would all have been blown up." These people, crowded around three middle-aged ladies with grenades, and the women themselves, of course, know what terrorists are like.

As a counterterrorist hunting and eliminating terrorists for fifteen or more years, I have looked terrorists in the eyes many times. In some instances, I saw a glint in their eyes when they thought my life was in their hands. I have also seen their eyes split seconds before I shot them.

As a counterterrorist I am foremost a highly trained and experienced specialist soldier. My enemies are terrorists of any nationality. My enemies are also those governments and people who give terrorists arms, money, and safe havens to train in and flee to. I have worked, almost always clandestinely, for the United States, Great Britain, Spain, and some of their allies. My missions have taken me to China, Iran, Greece, Africa, the Lebanon, and into less exotic strongholds of terrorists in Western Europe.

My alliance is with the victims of terrorism. My highly specialized job has been to prevent further victims, usually by killing terrorist leaders. What the reader of this book will have to decide is whether these terrorists are his enemies also, for there are ways of putting a stop to the terrorist war if we understand who these people are and if we clear away the semantic and ideological muck that has confused so many otherwise perceptive people.

A TERRORIST IS a male or female person, adolescent or adult, who willfully embarks on missions to kill or main persons usually unknown to him. In daily life most murderers kill people known to them. The terrorist capitalizes most on outrages in which people are killed at random in a department store they happen to be in when a bomb goes off or in an airport when a check-in or baggage area is sprayed with machine-gun fire or hand grenades. In conventional military actions, once fought by men alone, women and children have become ancillary victims, but to the terrorist women and children are direct targets, undifferentiated from men or perhaps even more attractive because of the particular horror that attaches, say, to the pointless death of an 11-year-old American girl or the wounding of her 9-year-old brother at the Rome airport just after Christmas 1985.

In the case of the kidnapping of the German businessman, Hans-Martin Schleyer, by the Red Army Faction, Schleyer's bulletproof car slowed down for what a witness described as a "lovely young couple" pushing a child's pram. Weapons for the assault were in the pram. Before Schleyer's driver realized the pram was a trick, his bulletproof car was blocked front and back by two terrorist cars and in moments Schleyer's three bodyguards and driver were all dead and Schleyer another kidnap victim who was eventually brutally murdered.

It is a mark of civilization to slow down instinctively in order to avoid hitting a baby carriage with a child in it, an instinct that the terrorist happily uses for his own ends. Using a child's pram or shooting a child is fair game precisely because the heart of the terrorist act is to spark anxiety in the hope of destabilizing society by making a great many people, reading their newspapers, watching their television sets, live in fear that the next terrorist act could happen almost anywhere, at any time, to anyone of any age. The fact is that if terrorists continue to win their sort of war, men and women living in civilized societies are an endangered species.

Contrast the effect of terrorist outrages with the murders committed by members of organized crime syndicates. We don't worry about them because they kill each other within a closed society. The terrorist kills us, us being anyone who happens to be at a location where an outrage is committed. If the terrorist struck only at his known enemies, he would not create terror.

FROM NEWSPAPERS AND TV it is easy to get the impression that terrorism is a largely male occupation. It is easy to forget that at one point in the seventies half of the most wanted urban guerrillas in West Germany were females. Ulrike Meinhof, one can recall, was the woman who shared the leadership of the most notorious terrorist group in Germany. The male half of the leadership, Andreas Baader, was a good deal younger, a handsome school failure who thought politics was for the birds. His game was bedding birds sequentially, but he was finally tamed into setting up housekeeping by a sexually very compatible young woman named Gudrun Ensslin, who was already turned on to "action" as the most desirable form of politics. It was Gudrun Ensslin who converted Andreas Baader from a playboy with no money and expensive tastes into a well-heeled terrorist, funded by rich sympathizers.

Anyone who has had contact with them knows that female terrorists are not Joans of Arc, nor are they comparable to the female maquis of the French resistance. Inge Viett, former schoolteacher, now a top member of the Red Army Faction, lives in Paris, where she drives around on a motorcycle. When a policeman stopped her for a traffic violation, she shot him dead and went merrily on her way.

The majority of female terrorists I've had to confront are spoiled, well-educated women from so-called good backgrounds who are turned on by aggressive acts. Some of them have first gotten involved in terrorist groups by becoming infatuated with a male terrorist or to prove themselves to a male-dominated society, as they see it, by being more macho than the men. In any event, they soon enough become single-minded, bitter killers. As terrorists, they are by and large very effective. They find it easier to infiltrate themselves into hostage-taking situations. And when they take hostages, they tend to intimidate male negotiators.

However, under pressure female terrorists will sometimes make the quick wrong choice, which can have dire consequences both for opponents, her partners, and innocent bystanders. Some who have investigated the phenomenon claim that a woman terrorist finds herself in an "unnatural" environment. (Ulrike Meinhof was the mother of two; you can't care for children when you're on the run or in hiding or preparing for an action.) The terrorist existence is often a lonely one. Cut off from normal sources of commendation, the terrorist's morale is dependent on her latest success. She lives in a world of violence and preparing for violence that was long thought to be a male preserve. Therefore there is great pressure for the female terrorist to keep proving herself. Under pressure, she will pass a point of no return, make a situation nonnegotiable. If she is the leader and feels she is losing control over the male terrorists in her command, outrage overtakes discipline. Sad to say, to preserve her status as an operative, she is more likely to kill children. She is also more likely to lose sight of the original objective of the mission and become suicidal.

Female terrorists make formidable interrogators of men. While they themselves are not humiliated to be stripped of their clothes, they know men are. And I know of one incident in which they forced their naked male prisoners to drink their own urine. Clearly, this is not the part of terrorism that gets TV coverage. Those of us who have to deal with them have to recognize that, as terrorists, women often have the drive to outdo their male companions in the ferocity of their acts.

THE NATURE OF terrorism is sometimes misunderstood because a terrorist group will often start out having a specific enemy. For instance, the ostensible enemy of the IRA has been the British government. On October 12, 1984, the IRA nearly succeeded in destroying the British government by means of a time-delay bomb planted in a Brighton hotel where the Prime Minister and her cabinet were staying. (I will show later why this particular IRA act failed and how it might have succeeded; after all, the IRA said, "We have to be lucky only once. You have to be lucky always.") But most of the time the IRA has Irishmen killing Irishmen, or women, or children, or, as in their bombings in London, passersby of any nationality. Their weapons are bought with funds supplied willingly or under duress by Americans of Irish extraction, which are mingled with funds whose source is Soviet or Soviet-controlled, such as Libya's. Does it seem strange that funds from the two antagonistic superpowers are mingled? That the IRA is linked with Arab, German, French, Italian, and Japanese terrorist groups? Such an amalgam does not seem strange to the counterterrorist who has seen most terrorist groups turn from their specific original goals into part of an international consortium of terror that has created a climate in which a minimum of force can accomplish major acts that terrorize millions.

Let's be specific. The United States, unprepared for war in 1941, was nevertheless able, with the help of its allies, to beat back the most powerful armed force ever assembled in Asia, fueled by religious and nationalist zeal; Japan's ordinary soldiers as well as their kamikazes were willing to die ostensibly to achieve the Greater East Asian Co-prosperity Sphere. The Japanese used terror methods, the bombing of civilian populations, the forced starvation of civilians, the death marches, the beheading of prisoners. But the United States, after the Japanese attacks against Pearl Harbor and the Philippines, was able to get its act together and win.

Yet that same country, reputedly the most powerful in the world, unprepared for terrorist warfare, was humiliated and paralyzed for fourteen months by the seizure of fifty-three of its personnel in its Teheran Embassy, a situation that could have been relieved quickly. One needs a certain mind-set to win a war. The United States is just beginning to develop the mind-set necessary to win the war the terrorists have begun. The European governments, having learned from hard experience, on the whole have a better approach to media handling, as their press and TV are generally more restrained.

Even a lesser terrorist act, the taking of TWA Flight 847, a terrorist hijacking that could have been dealt with swiftly and effectively, turned into a seventeen-day-long media event that humiliated the United States once again. What is this power that the terrorists have that enables so few of them to paralyze hostages, their families, their governments, and a world of onlookers?

In previous eras, a man filled with rage, possessing a weapon and a cause, as in the case of the nineteenth-century anarchists, could shoot or throw a bomb at a political leaders and send a shock wave through a community. It is only with the advent of worldwide news coverage and especially the instantaneous and visible coverage by television that an outrage committed in one place can terrorize not just the community where it took place but indeed the whole world. What we have now that is new is a *cost-effective* means of killing a small number of people and terrifying millions. The Arab terrorist, sinking to the floor in front of check-in counters at Rome airport moments before his death, can raise two spread fingers in a "V for Victory" sign because he knows that even if no camera was recording the actual massacre in which he just participated, the cameras and newsmen will be there soon enough to record the bodies and the blood and the police tags, a scene of carnage that hundreds of millions will see.

Another reason a comparatively small number of terrorists can cause such a cost-effective response is that we confuse terrorists with revolutionary armies and insurgent forces. Terrorists cannot be thought of as if they were governments. Diplomacy is the means by which governments deal with governments short of war. *Terrorists are fighting a declared war,* but we sometimes read their declarations incorrectly.

In April of 1985, two Belgian terrorist groups working jointly, the CCC (Cellules Communistes Combattante) and FRAP (Revolutionaries for Proletarian Action) continued a series of bomb attacks against various organizations that had symbolic significance for them. Their French allies, Action Directe, moved in and placed a massive car bomb outside the offices of the Belgian Employers Federation. Thirteen persons were injured in the explosion. Two who were killed were firemen trying to put out the resulting blaze. The stated motive of the car bombers was "A salute to international workers' solidarity against the exploiters." *Were the firemen the exploiters?*

In Italy when the Red Brigades assassinated American foreign service officer Leamon Hunt, they issued a statement saying, "No to all missiles, no to rearmament, Italy out of NATO." But Hunt had nothing to do with NATO. He merely resided in Rome. His task was to head the group that was supervising the Sinai agreements reached between Israel and Egypt.

When the Greek terrorist group, Christos Kassimos, failed in its attempt to blow up the German Embassy in Athens, it nevertheless issued a communique, saying, "The employment of any kind of force against the German State is a justified and humane act, and also an act of self-defense against its capitalist brutality." Another Greek terrorist group calling itself the National Front, bombed a night club in Athens frequented by American servicemen. Their message to the world: "The United States is responsible for the continuing occupation of Cyprus by Turkey"!

I learned long ago that terrorist communiques are basically *irrelevant* to their acts. Their real message is: Our outrages are meant to destroy your world.

What then is their world that is so opposed to ours?

TERRORISTS, LIKE OTHER subversives, tend to link up with their counterparts in and from other countries and cultures who also use terrorist means. The linkage, as will be shown in this book, is sometimes astonishing in the way it brings together Catholics and atheists, Christians and Muslims, Muslims and Communists, Orientals and Caucasians, whose ostensible causes may seem very different *except for the use of terrorist means.*

The means are important. In my work I have found that terrorists who plan and commit outrages become as inured to their work as surgeons do to cutting open human bodies (sometimes to repair the damage done by terrorists). However, the surgeon, who probably likes his work if he is good at it, has an end in mind, the curing of disease or countering the effects of trauma. The terrorist, who spends his time thinking of ways to create maximum trauma, begins to be fascinated by his work and to forget, over time, the original purpose he had in mind when he became a terrorist. If the layman cannot fathom that a terrorist actually begins to take sick pleasure from his work, he should recall the photographs of the killer of the Jordanian Prime Minister in the lobby of the Cairo Sheraton, kneeling to lick up the dead man's blood.

Laymen seem to have trouble understanding the process in which someone enlists with fervor in a cause and the fervor—and the action it entails—transforms itself into the goal. While it is true that some are originally attracted to violence and therefore to terrorism, the usual course is for a young person, male or female, to get involved in a cause, then feel frustrated because society does not respond fast enough to the demands of the cause, and finally to crave action against the society he sees as the enemy. Terrorism provides him with an outlaw action. He or she is now a bomb thrower, a kidnapper, a killer who cannot retreat to society and say "I'm sorry." In fact, the number who feel that way are very few, but the vast majority who have tasted the giving end of violence are caught up in the adrenaline high of taking human life, disrupting society, terrifying strangers, and seeing themselves and their group publicized in newspapers and on TV around the world. Instant stardom has always been a magnet. Terrorists become worldwide stars, and they find themselves on an emotional bobsled, their original motivation now reduced to irrelevant slogans. However, their life of self-denial and isolation leads some of them into the fantasyland of extreme paranoia, in a rage against their legendary enemies that can find release when their trigger fingers send bullets smashing into bodies.

In my experience, terrorism is addictive. Terrorists get to like their work more and more. They get a high from making plans for an outrage, they get a high from the actual commission of an act that immediately grabs the world's attention, and they get a high when important governments literally let them get away with murder and help their leaders escape the law.

To put it succinctly, the job of the government is to protect you anywhere in the world. The job of the terrorist is to make you feel unprotected everywhere in the world.

It is useful to note that the governments that sponsor terrorism (e.g. Iran, Libya, Syria, the Soviet Union) are not very protective of their own citizens. Iran's internal reign of terror has been directed at Iranians. Libya's hit squads abroad have targeted Libyan opponents of Qaddafi. Syria has induced young Syrians with personality or family problems to prerecord interviews for Syrian television before being sent off on what turn out to be suicide missions. Syria also regularly sends terrorist squads into Iraq to kill Syrian exiles. The Soviet Union has killed more of its own citizens in peacetime than has any other nation.

The planners of terrorist attacks know that the idea of "suicide squads" itself strikes terror into people who value their lives. And so they have successfully pushed the notion that Islam has an endless supply of young fanatics willing to blow themselves up in a holy war. In 1985 the Israelis managed to capture three suicide attackers before they could reach their targets. None of the three, according to Israeli officials, seemed to be religious fanatics; they did not even seem to be religious. Two of them—a sixteen-year-old boy named Mohammed Burro and a seventeen-year-old girl named Mayilla Soufangi—were not well-educated and seemed to have no clear-cut political ideas. The third, Mohammed Nasser, in his twenties, had been "volunteered" for his mission by a brother who didn't get along with him. Terrorist leaders are pretty cynical about the fodder they use.

Of course there are religious fanatics available to the planners of terrorism. These fanatics are quite ready to kill the infidel if they are pointed in the right direction, but they don't mean to get themselves killed in the process if they can help it. In fact, one doesn't have to be a profound student of Islam to know that the Prophet Mohammed disapproved of suicide. As a result, Islamic teachings hold that whatever the circumstances, someone who commits suicide is *barred* from paradise. Moreover, not only is the suicide consigned to hell, he is doomed to repeat over and over again the act in which he committed suicide. To be killed by the enemy in battle gets one to heaven, to destroy oneself reaps its punishment in hell. Islamic "suicide" is therefore a tool with which terrorist organizers both frighten their victims and mislead their own young.

Terrorism has been helped by the fact that in many places the public image of the terrorist is solely that of a fanatical, gun-toting Arab because that's what is most often seen on television. All the more when this is supported by dialogue that refers to the Qaddafis of this world as crazies. That image underestimates the deadly aims of the terrorist community and assists the survival of the more physically acceptable groups, such as the IRA. The fact is that many of the terrorists—including those who jointly perform outrages with the Arabs—look and sound like Europeans, which they in fact are. In appearance, it is impossible to distinguish white Anglo-Saxon IRA terrorists, or Spanish Basque ETA terrorists, or members of the white supremacist terrorist groups in America from ordinary citizens. When some horrible crime is committed, one sees on television the people from the criminal's neighborhood saying what a nice, quiet, ordinary chap he was. It is the same with the majority of European terrorists, who look like one's neighbors until they are pointing an AK-47 in one's face.

As a soldier in combat in Vietnam, I have had a grudging respect for my adversaries. They fought, usually bravely, on their own territory and against military targets. However, I have never felt an ounce of respect for the terrorists whose cowardice is exposed when they take their war to innocent civilians beyond the geographical borders of their cause.

Terrorism is of course a dangerous activity for the participating terrorists. Risks are high, and many can expect to die in the course of their work. However, the organizers and leaders of terrorist outrages do not themselves voluntarily give up their lives. It is the purpose of the counterterrorist to cause them to do so, to eliminate not only terrorist gunmen but most particularly terrorist leaders.

The word "counterterrorist" has been surrounded by as much semantic nonsense as "terrorist." As an active counterterrorist, I have been called a mercenary, an assassin, a killer, as well as a counterterrorist. Obviously, the air needs clearing and the term needs defining if counterterrorism is going to lead to a successful conclusion of the prolonged war that the terrorists are, at present, winning.

2

Countering Terrorism

You wouldn't want to see an amateur commissioned to build a bridge on which you expected to drive your car. Yet even the professionals who build bridges have seen their spans crack, fall, and kill people. The point is that you stand a much better chance with professional bridge-building engineers. Where lives could be threatened, you go with the professionals.

Many more lives are threatened by terrorism than by bridges. Yet much of the job of countering terrorism has been left to amateurs, with horrendous results.

First, let's take a look at the professionals. The names that have been slung at them are "mercenaries, assassins, killers." Hang those words in front of your eyes for a minute. They reek of negative assumptions. Yet each is in some measure a truthful description of what a counterterrorist is obliged to do.

A mercenary is someone who works for pay or other reward. That would seem to include most adults in most societies.

Today a mercenary is usually thought to be a hired

rather than a conscripted soldier who volunteers to serve a government *not his own.* The Vatican is guarded by Swiss mercenaries; though historic, they are better on parade duty than on guarding the pope against terrorist attack. When Americans fought the British in their Revolutionary War, their British opponents employed Hessian soldiers at so much a head. During the Renaissance, Italian *condottiere* hired out their troops to city states. Alexander the Great used mercenaries, as did the Romans.

The word "mercenary" has acquired a pejorative ring because the most famous mercenaries of the twentieth century were the men of the French Foreign Legion, who were usually on the run from the law, renegades with something on their consciences who were willing to endure the harsh discipline of an elite unit and the danger of death in a lost cause in a distant land. Whatever glamour may have attached to the Legion is to be found in old Hollywood movies and not in the real world.

"Mercenary" attached itself to the soldiers of fortune who fought in Africa under men like "Mad Mike" Hoare, seemingly for the money, the excitement, and perhaps a psychological attraction to combat and death that I will leave to others to explore.

I began my present career as a highly trained New Zealand soldier fighting in what many thought of as "America's war" in Vietnam. We Kiwis, as we were called, came from a small country with a population less than Libya's. (Libya has four million people, New Zealand three.) New Zealand is, like Australia, "down under," and what we are under is an Asia that was increasingly falling into Communist hands.

In Vietnam, I was assigned to a mixed-nationality Special Forces team that had the task of penetrating deep into the north, and across the Chinese border, to take out General Giap. The mission was aborted at the last minute because of political considerations. I, and the members of our small team, were considered expendable. I learned early that soldiering and political expediency do not mix well. Today, whenever they are mixed, the fight against terrorism falters. Today's terrorism is the result of past political expedience. Terrorism will continue to plague the world as long as our leaders kowtow to what's useful for the moment instead of the end goal: getting rid of the terrorists.

Since that time I have worked for many governments, usually covertly through agencies that can deny my existence. I will not work for any government that itself employs terrorists. Nor will I work for any communist government. For many years I did the dirty work—often disowned, it comes with the territory—of various NATO allies, including the seeking out and killing of terrorist leaders.

I have suffered two bullet wounds, one on each upper thigh. Much worse was the drastic injury to my left leg when I was just a few yards away from a "present" left by the enemy in the form of a jumping land mine. The surgeons were intent on amputating my leg. I told them that I didn't intend to leave the hospital one leg short.

One morning last summer I ran along the beach at Montauk, in the wet sand, for seven miles to buy a newspaper for a female friend. If the surgeons who had wanted to take my leg off could have watched, it might have given them pause before other operations. Medicine is a very inexact science, and though doctors have saved my life more than once, I am sure they have failed to save others more than they would have liked. In my occupation as a counterterrorist, I have to aim at a 100 percent success rate.

In the public media I have sometimes been referred to as a "killer." Some people are surprised to find that I am articulate because their mental image of a "killer" is that of a gangster or Mafia hit man. I am not a gun for hire. As a counterterrorist, I am a soldier not of fortune but of principle, and like fourteen million Americans who were trained as "killers" during World War II (some of whom were presumably articulate), I employ my special training for a cause I very strongly believe in. I want to defeat the terrorists who are conducting a successful war—successful especially against those nations that remain innocent of the terrorists' true motives. The United States is today the prime example of such innocence as well as the prime target for terrorists.

I HAVE BEEN asked publicly would I accept an assignment to kill Qaddafi. Not only ordinary citizens get this idea into their head. Back in 1981, the President of France, Giscard d'Estaing, and Sadat of Egypt conspired to assassinate Qaddafi, only to abort the plan later. The point of this foolishness is that Qaddafi is the known devil. We know where his arms come from. We keep pretty good track of where they go. If Qaddafi were killed, there would be at least a half a dozen or more lesser known devils jumping at each other to take Qaddafi's place, some of them much more pro-Soviet than Qaddafi, whose actions even alarm the Russians at times. There is a way to deal with Qaddafi's support of terrorism, which I will detail in Chapter 12.

The fact is that America, naive as it may sometimes seem, has long had an interest in professional counterterrorism, exercised covertly and deniable. Sometimes the activities of counterterrorist professionals are impossible to deny—for long. When the British SAS Pagoda Team reached London in preparation for storming the Iranian Embassy, their presence in the capitol was denied, but undeniably there they were, seen on television, dressed in black, including balaclavas to hide their identity and frighten their opponents, abseiling from the roof into windows, killing all but one of the terrorists and freeing the hostages with minimum harm. The professionals have long come to accept that in their specialized role they are persons about whom their own governments will talk out of both sides of the mouth. And that is perfectly agreeable, as is the fact that they risk their lives, as soldiers must, and kill efficiently, as soldiers must.

Which brings me to the discussion of a difficult matter for most people to consider objectively without turning into moral jelly, incapable of thought.

There are people on this earth who think of all life as sacred and who will not step on a roach. The fact is that roaches and their kindred insects have proved their ability to survive the centuries much better than man has. Similarly, rats have in every century outwitted mere men in survival techniques. To me, terrorists are like roaches and rats; if we let them proliferate, we will lose the war in which we have been pitted against them by their volition. They initiated the war against us, and not vice versa. Therefore, I remember hearing stories about captured SS killers who claimed immunity from prosecution because they were "only following orders." Moral mankind asserted that following orders to participate in the murder of innocent people is not an acceptable excuse. I remind my readers that terrorists are not following orders unwillingly. They are *volunteers*. And what they have volunteered to do is not to fight conventionally by adhering to Geneva conventions or whatever—they have volunteered to kill innocent bystanders and hostages in order to destabilize civilized societies.

A man will fiercely defend himself, his wife, his child from attack. Societies whose populations believe in them will defend themselves fiercely. Or they will hire counterterrorists to do their dirty work.

As a counterterrorist by conviction, my aim is to win the terrorist war by the best means available. These will be detailed in due course. My job has been not that of a strategist but of a tactician on the ground. And my function has been to kill terrorists. My rationale will be clear from the following example.

A few years ago I had an assignment in Spain. I was

advised in a briefing that two Basque terrorists were at a certain location, a private and otherwise unoccupied dwelling. I had to consider the following questions. If the intelligence information given me was incorrect, there might have been more than two terrorists in hiding in the "safe house" location. And I was given as my team two members of the Guardia Civil, who are law enforcement officers. I have the highest respect for good law enforcement officers around the world, but the fact is that only a very small number of them have had any training at all in dealing with terrorists, and those who have been trained have received instruction and practice at a level far lower than have the special forces such as SAS, Delta, GSG9, and their counterparts in other countries. Therefore it is most unusual for me to have to use policemen on an antiterrorist assignment, but in this case I had no choice.

The plan was for the two policemen to force their way into the front of the house. I stationed myself in a wide culvert at some distance from the rear of the house, where I could observe the back door and deal with an exiting terrorist, whichever direction he chose to take.

As it happened, one of the terrorists did flee through the back door and headed straight into the wide culvert in my direction. When he saw me, his first instinct was to reach for the gun in his belt while still running, but he must have seen that my gun was already in my hand and he changed his arm movements, raising them sideways. I must suppose that he might have raised his hands all the way up into the surrender position, but he lacked that opportunity because I shot and killed him. In most societies, a law enforcement official could be subjected to punishment for killing a criminal instead of taking him prisoner. But a counterterrorist must have a completely different mindset. This terrorist had killed innocents brutally. He had made his own rules. It is amazing how he and others like him expect a choice when the time comes to face the consequences of being a terrorist. *A terrorist who is allowed to live and goes to prison quickly becomes the direct cause of another terrorist act designed to free him.* The further act may—and frequently does—involve taking hostages and killing one or more as a demonstration of intent. Therefore the only way to stop the escalation of terrorist acts is to kill known terrorists, not take them prisoner.

The fact is that in the wars of this century, the taking of prisoners has been a matter of choice. Paratroop units of the Allies, jumping behind enemy lines, did not encumber themselves with prisoners. The enemy made similar choices. There are dozens of examples, extrapolating into hundreds of incidents, when it would have been a self-defeating act to take prisoners. The Western Allies in World War II had to deal with Japanese soldiers who were also fanatics; their suicidal code has been adopted by the present-day Japanese terrorists, and, as I have witnessed, the human wave attacks by the Iranian militia in their onslaughts against the Iraqis. The same fervor is demonstrated by the hordes of Islamic terrorists, whose creed includes self-extermination through death in a holy war. If you are raised by the ordinary standards of what we sometimes call "the Western world," you have a handicap in battle if you want to survive and the enemy doesn't care whether he does or not. In World War II a kamikaze pilot, willing to sacrifice his life, could take hundreds of seamen on a single ship with him. Similarly, a Japanese foot soldier holed up in a cave, willing to die rather than surrender, could kill many before he himself dies. Under such conditions, the taking of prisoners, Geneva Convention or not, became rather academic. The point of relevance is that *most terrorists are also fanatics.* Whether they are followers of the Islamic Revolution, or the Japanese Red Army Faction, or members of the successor organizations to the German Baader-Meinhof gang, they are fanatics willing to die in their attempts to terrorize populations and hold people hostage and governments at bay.

Hardened criminals have been known on rare occasions

to be freed from prison by other hardened criminals risking their freedom to set their colleagues loose. Terrorists have a great advantage over such criminals. They don't have to storm prisons, or land helicopters in prison yards, or smuggle guns past layers of prison security. They just have to take some innocents hostage and threaten to kill them unless their fellow terrorists serving prison terms are released. A terrorist in prison, I repeat, is an invitation to further terrorism, and until we understand that and act on it, our mind-set will not be ready to win that war.

If my job as a counterterrorist is to storm a plane, my only real chance of achieving success (freeing the hostages with a minimum loss of life) is to direct my action to the quick killing of the terrorists. I have very few seconds to complete my task. Common sense dictates that this is a military action in which kill or be killed applies. If a terrorist is wounded and survives, in some sense the counterterrorist act has failed because wounded terrorists are then protected by society and thus become the inspiration for further terrorist acts.

Counterterrorist professionals I have worked with and known are dedicated to careful planning to avoid the taking of innocent lives. I know of antiterrorist actions that have been postponed, putting the counterterrorist forces at greater risk, because the terrorists were mingling with others who were not terrorists.

I fully realize that some of the things I say in this book will be upsetting to many. So be it. My job is to tell the truth gained from my experience on the ground fighting terrorists.

The methods I describe in this book are known to the Soviets and are passed down to the terrorist groups they support. The people who orchestrate terrorist acts in Moscow and elsewhere are not ostriches. It's we in the West who are ostriches. Which leads me to the main reason I am allowing some of the material in this book to be published. *The public has a need to know.*

I am convinced that many members of the public in Britain, France, Germany, Spain, Italy, and elsewhere feel as I do about crushing the international terrorist enterprises. In 1985, when I was interviewed widely on TV and radio, I sensed a ground swell of support for counterterrorism. This book is designed to answer the important questions that are obviously on the minds of people of all nationalities, not just when they are boarding planes or mixing in large crowds, but when, in the safety of their armchairs, they are still concerned about their country being held to ransom whenever terrorists strike.

Most of my time is now taken up in working with law enforcement agencies that are developing expertise in dealing with terrorist activity. I also advise businesses with foreign and domestic operations that are especially susceptible to terrorist attack. But all of this specialized teaching will accomplish little unless the public itself understands the whys and wherefores of the terrorist war from someone who has been in the thick of it for the better part of two decades.

In sum, this book is for the people I have fought for—unbeknownst to them—most of my adult life. My intention is to deprive them of their innocence.

3

Amateurs and Professionals

If someone suggested you go after a hornet's nest with a fly swatter, you'd laugh. In fact most of the world has responded to the terrorist declaration of war with the equivalent: SWAT (Special Weapons and Tactics) teams and other somewhat specialized law enforcement officers whose experience, basically, is dealing with criminals and crazies.

Police hostage-negotiating teams are manned by experts trained in psychology who try, *however long it takes,* to talk the hostage taker into giving up his hostages and surrendering. Let's be very clear about this point. Terrorists are an entirely different breed. They are not alone, isolated by a cordon of police from the rest of the world. They are the committed frontline troops backed by an organization. Their organizations are backed by Iran, Syria, Libya, North Korea, the Soviet Union, and others. Their usual way is to kill at least one hostage early in the drama in order to prove they mean business (e.g., sailor Stethem, voyager Klinghoffer). And their intent is to stretch out the terrorist act for as long as possible because the objective is publicity. A criminal or a crazy does not strike terror into the rest of humanity. We are used to aberration striking somewhere once in a while. We are not used to being the constant targets of a war. And law enforcement officers, however able, are not soldiers and are not intended to be.

Even the FBI, the G-men of legend, do not yet have the mind-set to deal with terrorists. At this writing a forty-seven-man rapid reaction team of the FBI is being trained at Quantico, Virginia, to deal with terrorist situations. But their emphasis is on equipment. I don't mean to minimize the importance of sophisticated equipment, but it is the man who needs training first. One day the FBI may be able to deal with terrorist situations effectively, perhaps after each of the specialized officers can do what a trained SAS or Delta Force soldier can do. But that would mean turning at least part of the Federal Bureau of Investigation into a military organization, which would be roundly opposed by many. Law enforcement *investigates* and arrests. Counterterrorists get in, kill, and get out. It's a different occupation.

I CONSIDER THE SAS (the British Special Air Service) the best trained force of counterterrorist soldiers in the world. The American Delta Force is getting there. The German GSG9 is first rate and may lack only the depth of SAS experience over several decades. Most of the equivalent forces in other armies aren't equivalent at all. They've got a lot to learn. The SAS has trained specialist troops in other countries. How the SAS differs from normal soldiering—and its ability to take on extremely hazardous anti-terrorist assignments without qualms and, usually, with quick success—relates to the selection process and training.

It's a bit different from what your ordinary infantryman got in World War II or Korea or Vietnam. It's even different from the specialist Green Beret training. What the SAS looks for in its recruits is a mind-set, a kind of toughness of outlook rather than the exaggerated muscular superstructure of a fictitious Rambo. Also, the SAS tries to rule out fanatics of any kind, whether they are fanatical teetotalers or physical fitness freaks. The regiment is wary of rigid loners, but they do look for the self-disciplined individualist. That kind of man will fit well into a small team when teamwork is required. The man who is all teamwork—an attribute encouraged by some of the regular armed forces—is not always suitable for SAS work, which frequently involves hazardous duty away from the team. If he is separated from the others or the others are killed, he has to continue to function at his best ability on his own initiative.

Weirdos have a hard time even getting into the selection process because all one SAS instructor has to say is, "I don't like him," and the man's out. There is a definite chemistry among the men who pass. You wouldn't recognize one if you passed him on the street whilst he was wearing civilian clothes. You wouldn't turn your head because, unlike Rambo, he's of average build for a European man, far from an Arnold Schwarzenegger; in fact, he is unlikely to draw attention to himself in or out of a combat situation. You can't be more self-effacing than to wear a ski mask, get in, get out in minutes, and leave the cleanup to the civil authorities.

The SAS men I have known well have what I would call a certain adrenalin quotient. Outwardly calm, when energized they can suddenly become adrenalin-pumping stations, filled with energy and electricity and the will to use their skill. They are perfect for rapid response situations. They are the kind of person who, if the phone rings in the middle of the night and a recognized voice says, "Now," will be out of bed, dressed in a flash, and on his way. In the jungle or desert, instant alertness is a life-saving quality that all SAS men must have.

The SAS is also a meritocracy, which means rank

doesn't count. An officer from another branch of service volunteering for SAS training is reducing his status—and pay—to the lowest level, starting from scratch. Even when fully trained, each mission has a leader who may or may not be the officer among them. Merit and special skill count; nothing else. The SAS does not attract Colonel Blimps. It could attract someone like T. E. Lawrence who, after becoming a legend as Lawrence of Arabia, could reenlist as an ordinary airman.

Cowboys who can turn into cowards in action are among those who are ruled out in the rigorous training. Until recently, the number one or two officer at the SAS head-quarter and training depot at Hereford would greet recruits with a casual British, "It's nice of you all to come along. I don't suppose most of you will be with us for more than a few days."

Those days include a number of training rituals that are called, for good reason, the "sickener" factor. For instance, recruits are immersed in a gully that contains not only a sea of mud, but large quantities of sheeps' entrails. If you can't take that, you'll never be able to attack a terrorist training compound stealthily and take out a sentry by cutting his throat and making sure he's dead while his blood is spurting all over you and his alimentary canal opens onto your shoes.

SAS selection training involves such things as doing a forced march of fifteen to twenty miles and, just as you arrive at your destination, exhausted beyond belief, you see the trucks awaiting you drive away empty. The marchers are told they've got to go another ten miles. Many men drop out at that point. Those who don't will usually find the trucks waiting two miles down the road for the now smaller unit. One-third of the recruits are out by the first weekend.

After 21 days of muscle- and mind-tearing exercises starting at 4:00 A.M. and continuing nonstop till 10:30 P.M. or later, the survivors are ordered out on an endurance march that lasts twenty hours. The frequent rain in the Brecon Beacons where the training is done and the freezing, biting winds are just nature's addition to the man-made handicaps to the trainees. Only one man, however, has died on the endurance march, and that's because he was a bit older than average and decided to go it alone rather than stick with a small group.

Physical endurance is just part of it. The SAS teaches its recruits not only techniques of combat survival, but because of the covert operations they must pass interrogation survival. The interrogation resistance course consists of such pleasantries as a half hour in which every mean investigating trick is played out in rapid succession. Then comes an eight-hour period of constant interrogation, followed by a twenty-four-hour interrogation, interrupted only by the blindfolded trainee having his blindfold whipped off and being exposed to a horrendously bright electric light while the interrogation continues. That doesn't get you by. After twenty-four hours you are told the treatment will go on much longer, and then you are asked crucial questions you are not supposed to answer.

That isn't all. With your hands shackled, you are dropped partially into water for eight hours and *then* interrogated while you remain hooded and tied. Candidates are also tied to a wooden board and totally immersed in a pond for up to twenty seconds and, as they come up gasping for air, are asked "What did you say your regiment was?" They know it's training, but the fear of accidental drowning can be nearly as great as that of real drowning.

I have been told that I'm not much of a talker except among close friends. I think you'll find that true of most people with my kind of training. Part of it is to learn the opposite of what you were taught as a child, when you were applauded for every new word in your vocabulary. We are taught not to talk under the kind of conditions that make it difficult to open up in front of others.

In addition to learning how to survive interrogation by

the enemy, you are taught how to interrogate. In many armies, especially in the Middle East and the Orient, persons being questioned can undergo really brutal beatings and torture without breaking. But if you're dealing with hardened soldiers or terrorists, brutality will simply strengthen their will to resist. SAS trainees are taught how to use guile and elaborate bluffs to worm their way into the defenses of the person being interrogated. This was of great help to me when I participated in the interrogation of three North Korean female commandos who killed a dozen Iraqi officers before they were caught.

SAS training also includes methods of escape and evasion. There's a characteristic joke you hear about the SAS man being the one who walks backward in the snow so that anyone following him will head in the wrong direction!

The men being trained for SAS work have been, at first, self-selected. They think they have the mettle, and they know something about the SAS's tough training beforehand. Even so, and with large numbers weeded out in the first week, further dropouts result in only five to seventeen percent passing the course. That makes the training very expensive, for, on average, you are probably spending money training eight people for every one who finally becomes an SAS fighter.

Finally is the wrong word, for the rigorous training continues as long as the man lasts in the SAS. After the basics, the men who survive the brutal course get specialist training. This includes high altitude free-fall parachuting, dropping from 12,000 feet for one minute, accelerating to a terminal velocity of 120 miles per hour before opening the parachute. A man learns to do this with a short period of ground training. And then he has to jump with over a hundred pounds of equipment that makes his stability in free fall something to worry about, especially at high altitudes where his gear can ice up instantly. A very dangerous part of this necessary training is free falling into open water, a technique that was considered at the time of the *Achille Lauro* hijacking.

Can you imagine local policemen or any law enforcement officer going through this kind of training?

In the field, SAS men operate often in small groups of four. One of those has had to have special training in high speed Morse, which is far safer to use in covert operations than voice transmission. Another man needs to have more than a passing knowledge of the language of the country where the operation is to take place. And yet another has to have paramedic training far beyond that of the ordinary medical corpsman. He has to be able to do basic surgery in the field since a casualty evacuation, which is not always possible in any event, may also blow the security of a secret operation. If an arm needs amputating, one of the four is trained to do it well enough so that his comrade has a chance of survival until he can get to a medical facility.

And with regard to counterterrorist work, perhaps the most important ingredient in the SAS course is learning to perfect the use of an automatic pistol in close quarters. An SAS man must be able to hit a three-inch circle on a static target three times in less than three seconds. A single SAS man must be able to burst into a room in which there are several armed men and shoot each of them at least twice from up to twenty feet away with aimed shots from a thirteen-round 9-mm Browning automatic. The SAS man must also practice and perfect instant magazine changes and, to save his life, must know how to clear jams in split seconds. The great benefit of such training is especially seen in antihijacking operations in which the risk of hurting innocents is minimized because of the high degree of training of the rescuers—if they are SAS trained.

There are advanced training sessions for those who must evaluate new weapons and the kind of surveillance equipment that is so useful in antihijack work as well as in hearing what's going on in a terrorist-occupied building, as I have had to do in a country where my presence was illegal and my role would have meant instant death if I was caught by the terrorists.

SAS men are also trained in arts ranging from a locksmith's course to the use of foreign firearms (a necessity these days) and, at a later stage, operational planning and intelligence work.

Everything I have said about SAS training will serve to clarify many of the constructive points made later in this book. Counterterrorism is not a job for SWAT teams or other law enforcement groups that have only a fraction of the kind of tough training required of every single private soldier as well as noncommissioned and commissioned officers in the SAS and, increasingly, in GSG9 and the U.S. Delta Force. The training of infantry officers in Fort Benning used to be called "eighteen weeks of hell in Georgia." Consider that this is only a portion of what SAS men volunteer to go through. FBI agents and SWAT team police officers are not put through the "sickener" factor that enables men to engage in close quarter combat and succeed every time. All of this highlights the need for highly and specifically trained teams.

AFTER A DECADE and a half of participating in many small team operations at great risk, I still support the basic traits the SAS looks for in its recruits. My experiences over all this time make me focus on certain extra qualities in the kind of men I prefer to take with me on dangerous missions.

I prefer what I like to think of as a self-contained individual with a strong spine and no need to lean on others. That takes self-confidence, which, of course, increases with experience; but the core of it has to be there from the start.

Selfishness has no place in covert operations. I had to weigh up the thought of shooting a member of our team in Iran when he chose to act in his own interests as against the interests of the group. A man has to be willing to submerge his ego in a cooperative operation in which everyone's life depends on everyone else.

I like members of my team to be logical and objective thinkers, not people who respond to internal pressures of personality. Admittedly, this characteristic is hard to come by. I've been lucky.

A man has to be willing to accept criticism without going into a sulk. Anyone qualified to come on one of my missions will already have proved himself able to take criticism.

The mind-set of the individual is very important. He should be able, no matter what difficulties the mission encounters, to keep his mind on the objective and not get sidetracked. I have seen men die because, beset by difficulty, they lost sight of the end goal.

There's a difference between being physically fit and strong. Strength may be good for the short haul or a specific event, but what I want in an operative is endurance. Without endurance, I'm certain I would have been dead a long time ago. I'm not too concerned about a man's age. It's experience and attitude I look for, and somehow, as the years go on, those qualities seem to improve in people who've had them in the first place.

And the last character I want on a mission with me is someone with a gung ho John Wayne syndrome. It may be fine for the movies, but in real life-threatening situations, that kind of attitude can endanger all the people on the mission. I want an individual who is composed under duress. And, most of all, who is driven not by bravado but by a genuine desire to achieve excellence. Because on our missions, excellence is not eighty percent or ninety percent but one hundred percent.

THE INEPTNESS OF civilian law enforcement dealing with a terroristlike situation was dramatically conveyed to the world in 1985 when a small group of eccentric revolutionaries, who call their organization Move, barricaded them-

selves in a row house in Philadelphia and built a bunker to
protect themselves from ordinary police weaponry.

Residents of the neighborhood claimed they had been
threatened by Move members, who were trying to pressure
Philadelphia officials to release some of their members
who were in prison as a result of a confrontation with
police in 1978 in which one policeman was killed and four
others, plus four firefighters, were injured. The authorities
were convinced that any try at taking the Move members
into custody would lead to violence. It would have been
easier to take the row house a year earlier, before it had
been fortified.

A panel that later probed the May 1985 assault asserted
that the adult residents of the Move house had held the
neighborhood "hostage." It said, "The residents of 6221
Osage were armed and dangerous and used threats, abuse
and intimidation to terrify their neighbors and to bring
about confrontation with city government." These Move
people can be called messianic madmen or subversive
fanatics, but they are not terrorists. Yet they were dealt
with with the same blockbuster psychology that caused
the failure of the American attempt to liberate its fifty-
three hostages in the Teheran Embassy by sending an
armada. Of course what the law enforcement people did in
Philadelphia, bombing the building and burning down the
entire neighborhood, was the supreme example of over-
reaction at work. Within an hour and a half, the police fired
10,000 rounds of ammunition, despite the fact that children were known to be in the house. The use of military
explosives by the police started a fire that was allowed to
burn as a "tactical weapon"! It resulted in the worst residential fire in Philadelphia's recent history, destroying no
fewer than sixty-one houses and leaving something like
250 people without homes. Inside the Move house, six
adults and five children were dead. You'll see what I mean
by overkill, if you stop and think that the relief of the
Iranian Embassy in London, a multistory building, was

accomplished by six well-trained members of a rapid response SAS team. My point is that counterterrorists can sometimes be useful in nonterrorist situations, but the reverse is not true: most law enforcement people, even in great cities like Philadelphia, are not equipped to deal with a small group of crazies, much less with dedicated terrorists.

The kind of rapid response team I have worked with, whatever the nationality, would have dealt with the Philadelphia problem in the following manner. The houses on the street would have been evacuated as quietly and quickly as possible. There would be no flashing lights of police cars or any other vehicles visible to the barricaded Move people. There would be no visible authority. The press would have to be kept away from the immediate area. Audio and visual surveillance of the interior of the Move-occupied house would be accomplished in the same manner as in hijacked airplanes on the ground, thus enabling the assault team to see and hear what was going on inside the house. The purpose, of course, would be to determine the location of the people inside and especially to distinguish between the armed persons and the children. While rapid response teams prefer to act quickly, because of the presence of innocent children, they would wait until the children were likely to be isolated, that is, put to bed. Electricity to the house would be cut off. So would the gas. The phone line would be kept open to allow protracted negotiations to wear down resistance and provide an opportunity for surrender. That was not likely, given the circumstances, but the possibility has to be kept alive until the assault team is ready. Five men trained to SAS or Delta Force standards could have covered the Philadelphia house in forty-five seconds to one minute. The armed people would have been shot or disabled. The women, if not armed, and the children would be moved out. The assault team would withdraw, leaving the law enforcement people to move people back into the neighborhood. No fire. No deaths of innocents. No burning down of sixty-one houses, leaving 250 people homeless. No citywide shame. No flare-up of racial antagonisms. Just an efficient—and by SAS or Delta standards—relatively easy operation. Local law and order had failed to evaluate the level of the crisis and had been too obstinate to call for outside help.

TERRORISTS HAVE ALSO displayed incompetence. I was in the airport at Barcelona with a lady. My companion and I were flying to Geneva on business. My Spanish assignment was over and the last thing in the world I wanted to think about was terrorists. After an operation I welcome a return to the mundane.

The lady and I had passed through Spanish customs and settled down in the airport departure lounge, a large space that includes the duty-free area. Our flight was reported delayed because of air traffic over France.

The departure lounge is patrolled by the Policia Nacional, which is the equivalent to the bobby on the beat in London or the patrolman on his beat in any American city. Outside the departure lounge, on the terrace overlooking the tarmac, as in other higher security areas, the patrolling is done by members of the Guardia Civil, who are more of a paramilitary force and more highly trained than the Policia Nacional in their ability to cope with emergencies.

We were in the lounge for about fifteen minutes, chatting, when my attention was caught by some activity over at the security passageways near the entrance to the departure lounge. There were a group of people who were late for their flight, which gets them tense and gets the security people even more tense. One Arab-appearing character seemed to attract the most attention because of his bumbling eagerness to make his flight, and he was escorted behind a screen. I learned later that the man's bag, when he was forced to open it, revealed in the neighborhood of a million dollars of U.S. money in bills, and atop the money was a gun. The man's ticket showed that

this courier had come off a flight from Algeria. It turned
out that he was transporting money for terrorists on the
continent.

Realizing he was caught, the Arab let out the kind of
piercing Arabic wail similar to what Arab women are
prone to release at funerals. It may have sounded like grief
to the Policia Nacional, but to me it was clearly a signal to
another terrorist that he had been caught.

Just then we heard an announcement that our flight to
Geneva would be delayed another forty-five minutes. This
was a calculated ploy by the Spanish authorities. I looked
around the lounge and spotted another Arab, a tall good-
looking fellow, wearing a lime green suit and brown shoes.
Not exactly inconspicuous!

His partner caught, he must have sensed that he was
possibly under surveillance and alone. Clearly his nerve
cracked, and he headed for the security-screening area
with the intent of leaving the departure lounge. I could
hear him saying in bad Spanish that he had no Spanish
money and wanted to go out to buy a drink. Instead, the
security people invited him behind the same screen where
his partner had been exposed. I observed a plain-clothes
policeman watching him, when suddenly the man panicked and made a run for it back into the departure lounge.
The plain-clothes policeman lunged for him and missed.
The Arab was running straight in my direction, just
behind the row of seats my friend and I were sitting in.

I guess that when something of that sort happens my
response is automatic. I stood on the seat ready to go over
the back of it and intercept the Arab. As I punched out at
him, my leg got caught between the back of the chair and
the seat. It was like a Buster Keaton comedy. My friend
grabbed at me, trying to keep me from breaking the leg
that was wedged in the chair. By this time my help wasn't
needed. A small mob of police had jumped on the kicking,
scratching, biting Arab. That was when I saw an over-

weight policeman draw his .357 magnum—probably for the first time in his life from the way he was handling this piece of heavy artillery—and hold it at head level at what seemed like one inch from my nose. I could swear his finger was twitching. After all my hazardous duty, I thought I was about to have my head blown off by a nervous policeman who was as incompetent as the two Arabs. With my lady friend still holding on to my legs, I tapped the policeman on his shoulder and said, *"Por favor, muy tranquil,"* which means something like *Please take it easy.* If he had fired that cannon, I swear *someone* would have been killed—and not the Arab in the lime green suit, who was now on the ground under a pile up of excited Policia Nacional.

The Guardia Civil could see and hear the commotion through the glass but remained at their posts outside, prepared but recognizing that inside was a different jurisdiction.

When they frisked the Arab in the lime green suit, he had a .225-caliber pistol on him, which confirmed my doubts about the technological quality of the metal detector he presumably passed through to get into the departure lounge. It was not clear why these two couriers were carrying weapons onto the aircraft. They should have left the weapons on the Algiers flight if they needed them to protect the money they were carrying in Algeria. One thing is certain: they were lacking experience.

We learned that the two Arabs were actually headed for Geneva on the same flight we had booked. This information was turned over to the counterterrorist network and led to the arrest in Geneva of two Swiss lawyers who were waiting for the couriers.

In retrospect, the whole incident seems comical to me: the inept terrorists caught by the inept police, with specialist Gayle Rivers' leg stuck in a chair at the critical moment.

After our Geneva visit, my lady flew back to Barcelona,

and I flew to Heathrow in Britain. In more recent times, I would not be all that confident of the British police who, as if on a war footing, now patrol Heathrow with automatic weapons. To satisfy public opinion, those weapons have been fixed so that they can only fire one shot at a time. If British policemen, after all those legendary years of going around unarmed, now have to carry machine pistols at the airport to give passengers a feeling of confidence, they would be sad targets for terrorists carrying AK-47s that fire on full automatic. The tragicomedy is that you can't fight terrorism with window dressing. It's not a job for policemen, whose primary care is public safety, but for highly trained soldiers prepared to cope with terrorists.

TO UNDERSTAND WHAT to do about relieving a hostage crisis, it is useful to look at the faults of one that got thoroughly mucked up. There are few better examples worth our attention than the so-called Iranian hostage crisis, which began on November 4, 1979, when a mob of armed Iranians seized the American Embassy compound, took fifty-three hostages, and subjected the Americans to fourteen months of humiliation and shame.

The rescue attempt, which did not take place till nearly a half a year after the hostage taking, was code-named Operation Eagle Claw. It amazes me how little the public knows about *why* the operation failed and how it might have succeeded. The "Claw" was blunted by dithering leadership in Washington and bureaucratic over kill.

The official version, announced by President Jimmy Carter, was "equipment failure." That's like blaming road accidents on faulty cars instead of inexperienced drivers. Machinery can't talk back.

First off, Operation Eagle Claw's planners ignored the basic rule for covert operations: Get in and out *fast*. The rescue plan involved American military personnel being in hostile territory for almost two days. Even the Joint

Chiefs of Staff gave it only a sixty to seventy percent chance of success, which to a professional reads like a thirty to forty percent chance of failure. Two to one odds are better than you get in a gambling casino, but military rescue operations should be worked out so as to have a much better chance for the assault team and the hostages getting out alive.

The key to special forces operations is that the group trains together. The gargantuan task force assembled by the Americans from air, sea, and land services never trained together in the Western U.S. desert training area that approximated some of the conditions that would be encountered in Iran. A force was built up from scratch with a new command-and-control system, creating an untried organization instead of using an existing one. Moreover, a task force consisting originally of eighty men ended up ballooning to over 250 men, of which no fewer than 132 were to be airlifted to Desert One, the first—and as it turned out last—stop on the mission.

A CIA plane had scouted the location to plant remote-control beacons to guide incoming aircraft. During the hour or so it took for the men on this secret mission to do their work, six vehicles drove by on a nearby road. That should have alerted all concerned that the location was wrong. You don't bring in a force that large that close to a traveled road. When the operation was underway, a busload of Iranian civilians came along and had to be detained. Moreover, a fuel truck that came along later refused to stop and was set on fire by an antitank round. The resulting blaze lit up the surrounding sky. They were probably gasoline smugglers and thought the Americans were Iranian police. The busload of Iranians who arrived later presented a real problem. When the helicopters had to be abandoned, they contained all sorts of secret documents that the Iranians later captured. These documents showed safe houses for U.S. secret agents, photos of places such as

the warehouse that hid the trucks that were to bring the
rescue force from Desert Two, close to Teheran, to the
Embassy compound, and radio call signs and frequencies.
After the abort, when President Carter had the option of
ordering in fighters from the aircraft carriers to blow up
the helicopters, he declined to do so because he didn't want
to endanger the Iranian bus riders detained at the location!
Good planning would have called for each of the helicopters to have been pre-rigged with self-destruct explosives.
A decade earlier, when the Americans sent an operation
to Son Tay in North Vietnam to release U.S. prisoners
thought to be held there, the helicopter crews had taken
steps to rig their machines with self-destruct explosives; so
the idea wasn't new. It was just that nobody thought of
implementing it in all those months of planning.

Indecisiveness and procrastination are not recommended for any relief assault, yet Colonel Charles Beckwith, the man in charge of the planned storming of the
Embassy compound, was told *no less than seven times* to
get ready to go. Now Charlie Beckwith, whom I know and
admire, is a first-rate soldier, but how can anyone function
effectively at the sharp end when such indecision reigns in
the high command.

The biggest fault in the operation was the communications planning. In order to preserve secrecy—a necessity in
covert operations—radio communication was barred between the aircraft and from the aircraft to the command
post on the aircraft carrier *Nimitz,* from which the eight
Sea Stallion helicopters took off. There are ways in which
the helicopters could have communicated without giving
the show away, but the ban on *any* communication—even
in emergencies—was the chief cause of the failure of the
operation. Let's look at what happened.

The first to abort was helicopter 6 about two hours into
the 600-mile flight to Desert One. A cockpit warning light
indicated a condition that might have meant a rotor blade
failure. The cockpit signal, known as a BIM (blade inspec-

tion method), caused the pilot to set the helicopter down. Helicopter 8 saw helicopter 6 set down, and went down alongside and picked up the crew. Now those of us who fly know that very often when we get a warning light in the cockpit, the problem is in the warning light system and not in the system that it's warning us about. In the case of the BIM signal, after the fact, it was shown that in 38,000 flight runs not one crack ever showed up in the type of helicopter used on this mission despite *three BIM signals.* Had the pilot been trained to have a more combat-oriented mind-set, he might have pressed on after rapid ground-checks and decided not to abandon his machine. Even if he was out of the mission, he might at least have made an effort to return to the ship. Worst of all, however, was the fact that he couldn't even use his radio to notify the mission command that they were already one helicopter short.

Pilots are used to being in close touch with weather forecasters. On this mission, because of excessive secrecy compartmentalization, the chopper pilots received an incomplete weather briefing and had no warning of the huge sandstorm they suddenly flew into. The pilots chosen for this mission had insufficient training for long-distance instrument flying and had a hard time dealing with the conditions they encountered.

Just a few minutes before clearing the sandstorm, Colonel Pitman, in command of chopper 5, saw an alarm signal indicating that a cool air blower to the chopper's power supply had overheated. Its failure made navigation and flight control systems operate erratically or not at all. Allegedly the trouble was traced to a crew member putting his flak jacket and duffel bag over the cooling vent, and this caused the motor to burn out! Lack of training and discipline on the part of the crewmen and the absence of a goal-oriented, press-on combat attitude resulted in robbing the force of another helicopter. Colonel Pitman, now knowing that he was almost in the clear because of the communications blackout, turned back into the sandstorm and headed for the aircraft carrier. That left only six choppers for Colonel Beckwith, who was getting impatient at Desert One because of the late arrivals caused by the sandstorm. Beckwith had said from the start that six was the absolute minimum needed for getting to Desert Two, the second stop just outside Teheran.

The last of the six choppers to arrive at Desert One was helicopter number 2. Then there was a case of real equipment failure. About two hours after it had taken off from the *Nimitz*, chopper 2 knew that there was a defect in the hydraulic system. As every pilot knows, there is a backup hydraulic system, which is why chopper 2 had been able to ride through the sandstorm and arrive at Desert One, albeit eighty-five minutes late. As soon as they got on the ground, the crew looked for the hydraulic problem and found a crack in a nut. Even if a spare hydraulic pump was available—and it wasn't—there would not have been enough time to install it and complete the mission before daylight. Colonel Beckwith, a man of action, had to make the painful decision to abort the entire mission because he was down to five helicopters and he himself had set the minimum at six.

It was after the decision to abort that in the course of refueling, in the noisy bedlam of Desert One, one of the choppers sliced into a C-130 on the ground, causing a massive fire that cost the lives of five airmen and three marines.

Within twenty-four hours of the abort, the hostages had been scattered to hiding places away from Teheran, and, for all practical purposes, were no longer rescuable. Khomeini's humiliation of the United States could continue for another nine months.

The failure of Operation Eagle Claw was in truth partly due to mismanagement of Operation Rice Bowl, the training part of the operation that stitched together a potpourri of military services that had not practiced the operation together; partly the failure to use available means of communicating in emergencies under combat conditions; and, of course, the basic plan, which involved too many people doing too much and doing it far too late.

Stupidity was even evident in such "minor" matters as the best set of floor plans of the American Embassy compound in Teheran being locked up in the embassy safe! Fortunately, a not-so-good second set of plans of the embassy buildings and grounds was available outside Iran.

It can now be revealed that in the first few days of the embassy takeover a group of specialists conceived of a workable plan to free the hostages. It would have involved only a small group of expert counterterrorists and not a major task force.

Before the seizure of the embassy, back in May and June of 1979, I personally led a small team into Khomeini's Iran to rescue two hostages.* The mission was dangerous but successful. When I, along with the rest of the world, heard of the takeover of the embassy, a number of counterterrorists got together and formulated a plan for the rescue of the fifty-three hostages.

First you must know that a sewer pipe that led out of one side of the embassy compound was large enough to accommodate a small group of men infiltrating one at a time. On the directly opposite side of the compound was a street, on the other side of which was a garage. The below-street-level part of the garage extended halfway across the street in the direction of the embassy. So the only digging that would be required for a two-pronged entry into the compound would be halfway across one street, a task that the SAS, Delta, and the like are quite competent to take on.

Moreover, it is important for the reader to know that the Delta team had people on the ground in Teheran. One of the best operators recruited by Beckwith was Richard J. Meadows, a retired major who was in Teheran in the guise

---

*This operation is described in detail in *The Teheran Contract,* by Gayle Rivers and James Hudson, Doubleday, Garden City, New York, 1981.

of an Irish businessman but was actually a U.S. covert agent who went about renting a warehouse and doing such necessaries as buying the trucks that Colonel Beckwith was supposed to use to move his assault force from Desert Two to Teheran.

The West has other people on the ground in Teheran. Some helped me in my prior mission. We had ways of contacting them. As a result we knew we could have transportation available to load the hostages and the assault force into. Because the Carter Administration had previously unwound CIA covert operations in Teheran, there was no U.S. underground network to support the operation, but covert counterterrorists had their own support network there.

One problem was the large number of Iranian student guards. The second problem was the hostages' own mindset, which made some of them identify with their captors; they might have put up some resistance to being herded out of the Embassy. Our advantage consisted of surprise, knowledge gained from our people on the ground, and the experience of specialist forces in the seventies in successful relief actions such as at Entebbe and Mogadishu.

I had had the experience of flying an aircraft in and out of Khomeini's Iran successfully. The thought of the planning group was that a light plane or commandeered Iranian helicopter, traveling by a rather roundabout route, could, with proper timing, arrive over the Embassy compound and drop stun grenades to take care of the guards outside, which would be the cue for the two squads coming in from the garage tunnel and the sewer pipe to storm the buildings and take out, as the Pagoda Squad did in London, the Iranian guards inside, who would of course not know whether they were being attacked from the air as well as the ground by a force much larger than themselves. At least the force would be noisier and more expert in close-quarter combat than the student militants. According to our calculations, the buses with the hostages aboard could have been 150 miles away from the Embassy before the Iranians got their act together for hot pursuit. At an agreed location, the planes that dropped the stun grenades (it was possible that two planes might be used in the initial action), and one other, a Lockheed C130 painted with Iranian air force markings, would rendezvous outside Teheran, pick up the hostages and the assault team (and possibly the Iranian bus drivers if their cover was blown), and head for either the Persian Gulf or the Mediterranean via Iraq.

No one can guarantee the success of an operation of that sort, but to experienced counterterrorists it seemed no more difficult than many other operations except for the somewhat larger number of people involved. The plan was put forward to Washington. I have no knowledge as to whether President Carter himself or an aide vetoed it on the ground that it wouldn't be a wholly American operation.

Terrorism is a multinational operation requiring a multinational response. Even at Mogadishu, the German GSG9 commandoes "borrowed" two British SAS stun grenade experts, who were the first to enter the plane. As soon as the Brits had got off their grenades, momentarily blinding and stunning both the terrorists and their hostages, they fell to the floor to serve as a human bridge for the GSG9 troops that killed the terrorists. Of course, when one read about it in the newspapers there was no hint of "international cooperation." As usual, the SAS, which like other specialized groups considers all terrorists to be the enemy, snuck in and snuck out, their expertise well used.

IT IS TIME now to take a realistic look at the specter of terrorism that most haunts laymen: the hijacking of an airplane and the taking of hostages. It's a subject about which the public has heard a lot of ill-conceived analysis and speculation.

4

The Truth about
Skyjacking

There were some 690 terrorist attacks in 1985, of which only a very small proportion were skyjackings. But I will deal with skyjackings straight off because they are so front and center in the public mind. Also, skyjackings become huge media events more than most hit-and-run terrorist attacks. If not dealt with swiftly, they can stretch over days or weeks while much of the world watches.

I first piloted a plane when I was sixteen and briefly held a job as a crop duster. Since then I have learned to fly jets, as I have had to do on some of my more difficult assignments in the Middle East. I also pilot helicopters, which can be very useful in counterterrorist operations. I feel comfortable in the air, but most people don't. Their fear of flying may contribute to their present fear of being hijacked in the sky.

When a fear of flying is compounded by the fear of being kept prisoner in a hijacked airplane, suddenly the possibility of man-made death is added to the natural fear of flying, and we have fear compounded. Which is exactly what hijackers relish.

Moreover, both for holidays and business, air travel is becoming the only effective means of getting to many parts of the world, so the reluctant air traveler has no choice. And with the threat of hijacking, he feels himself to be in double jeopardy.

On television I have been asked questions like, "Do you ever go armed on commercial airlines?" The fact is that to do so would be an unnecessary nuisance as in my work I have arranged to pick up at my destination whatever weapons I may need for my own safety or for an assignment. In some cities, I have permanent arrangements that enable me to be armed on land without violating airline rules. But the truth is that as a counterterrorist, I can have my weapons escape detection just as easily as any terrorist can.

Security measures taken at airports, I am sorry to report, are largely insufficient. Let me demonstrate.

The first concern of airline security procedures is to see that the passengers don't bring weapons or explosives aboard. That is why individuals have to pass through a metal-detecting frame and put their carry-on luggage on a belt that passes through an X-ray device or is opened and inspected by the eye and hand of a trained security person.

Both the metal-detecting and X-ray devices are instruments whose sensitivity can be turned up and down. If the frame the airline passenger walks through is kept at its most sensitive, a couple of coins or a piece of jewelry will set it off. Hence, for practical reasons of passenger flow, the sensitivity is kept at a level that will detect a large metal object like a gun, knife, or sharp-pointed screwdriver, which can be used as hand-held pseudobayonet. The detection device will also be set off by a pocketful of change, or a metal pillbox plus some keys on a ring, but most airlines will accommodate passengers by having them put these objects in a plastic tray before they pass through, and the tray is then passed around the side of the metal-detecting portal.

But what good are X rays or metal-detecting portals against bombs made of plastic that weigh as little as a pound, yet are powerful enough to blow a hole in the fuselage of an airplane in mid-flight, as one did to TWA's Flight 840 when it was ten minutes away from landing in Athens on April 2, 1986, with the resulting decompression sucking four Americans out into thin air. Plastic can be molded to any shape. What's to keep a terrorist from molding it to the shape of any familiar object that a passenger might have in carry-on luggage? And timing devices and detonators now come so small that they can be easily hidden within familiar objects and in any event will not throw off an alarming shape on the security screen.

More secure airports (not necessarily the most vulnerable) will have passengers frisked. That is time-consuming, sometimes embarrassing, and not at all foolproof. A trained person (not all friskers are well trained since few of them are law enforcement people) will run his hands down both sides of your torso, both sides of each arm, and both sides of each leg up into your crotch. If a frisking is not that thorough, the airline employee is likely to miss, for instance, the kind of armament I frequently carry (though not aboard airplanes), an ankle holster with a gun on the inside of the lower leg. Rarely do friskers check *the center of the back,* yet it is very easy to carry a knife suspended *down one's back* from a leather thong or a decorative chain around the neck. Even very experienced friskers will not detect a flat automatic pistol (not a revolver) that is taped just above the pubic bone on a man or a woman.

And no metal detector is going to go off if a hijacker takes as a weapon of choice an Austrian-made Steyer 9-mm high-powered semiautomatic whose parts are made entirely of plastic!

Even the X-ray machines that "see" the outlines of objects within bags carried aboard will not make much of the parts of a disassembled gun, particularly if the parts are separated into more than one bag and carried aboard by two or more of the hijackers.

When 300 or 400 people are to board a single wide-bodied jet, it is destructive of the convenience of air travel to subject each such person to the kind of carry-on luggage examination and body search that would be more foolproof than the methods used today. And for busy airports, where the majority of terrorists have boarded, with jumbos being loaded frequently, devoting even ten minutes per passenger would bring air travel to a standstill.

Add to that the burden of legitimate passengers with special problems. One of my friends wears a metal frame brace when traveling either by car or plane to minimize the vibration in his damaged spine. The brace is large and goes from his neck to the top of his buttocks. Since the brace would undoubtedly set off the metal detector at security checkpoints, my friend removes the metal brace before going through security and passes it around the detector to the man or woman monitoring the machine and gets it back on the other side. Not one such "security guard" has ever examined this large metal brace, which is hollow and could easily contain one or more stilettos or the crucial parts of a disassembled gun.

Another man whose work intersects with mine in non-covert activities was more severely injured in Vietnam than I was. He was on a Honda motorcycle just behind a jeep, both of them headed north, when they saw an armored personnel carrier headed south toward them at full speed in the wrong lane and the road narrowing at a bridge just ahead. The jeep speeded up and made it off the bridge in time, but the South Vietnamese armored personnel carrier hit the motorcycle just as my friend stood up ready to jump off the bridge to escape the inevitable collision. The impact of the armored car sent him flying upward and over the speeding personnel carrier. The pilot's helmet he was wearing split in two but saved his skull. Every long bone in his body was broken. He was in hospital for three years between 1966 and 1969, and suffered through thirty-five operations in twenty years. He can now get about well enough, though one can tell that he must have been badly injured once. His body, particularly at the joints, is held together with parts that set off the metal detectors at airports. He used to carry a medical ID with his picture on it to avoid problems whenever he set off the alarms. Since those IDs can be faked, he no longer is allowed one, which means that at airports with tight security, such as in Dallas and Minneapolis, he is body-searched when he travels within his own country.

There are thousands like him who travel by air frequently and who are exposed to great inconvenience. Obviously, the metal-detecting devices and X-ray machines in common use at most airports are of some value, as is the frisking that is employed much less often. It is true that literally thousands of illegal weapons have been confiscated since these security measures have been put in place, but when was the last time it was reported that an actual terrorist had been caught because of a metal-detecting device or an X-ray machine or a frisking?

Similarly, the so-called "terrorist profile," used by airline personnel at check-in counters and at aircraft gates, is more of a public relations exercise than a useful tool. The profile is derived from past-known terrorists. Airline personnel looking for the profile might well miss the terrorist, as in the Egyptair hijacking of November 23, 1985, when the leader of the hijack gang was said to be extremely well dressed, like a businessman. The fact is that the airline employees who use the "terrorist profile" are not well trained and kept up-to-date on potential terrorist activity, nor could such a large army of civilians be exposed to the intelligence information that has been the main source for blocking terrorist acts.

BUT EVEN IF metal detectors, X-ray devices, and frisking worked perfectly, which they do not, consider the case of

TWA Flight 847, which was hijacked out of Athens on June 14, 1985. The weapons the hijackers used weren't brought aboard by them. They were already on the plane, stowed in a lavatory by *ground personnel*. This means, of course, that security measures must be extended to all persons who approach or enter an airplane, not just passengers. Cleaners, mechanics, and others need to have their persons, tool carriers, and garbage collection bags inspected before they approach any airplane. To be effective, ground crew and cleaners would have to be checked many times each day because, as they go in and out of the terminal before and after servicing each plane, they could easily pick up stashed weapons from their lockers or other hiding places at any time during their workday.

Persons concerned with the economy of airline transportation could, with justice, protest the cost of frequent reexamination of ground crew daily. Ground personnel would not stand for it, and the employers could maintain, as many do, that they check the backgrounds of employees, and members of the ground crew must wear ID tags as they move about the airport. The truth is that airport ID is no harder to come by for a determined terrorist than fake passports. Moreover, pressure can be exerted on a perfectly *previously* reliable employee to carry material aboard by simply advising him of the danger that might come to his family if he doesn't cooperate. Also, it is not only in the poorer countries that people can be tempted by money alone to "do a little something," like taking a plastic bag aboard and leaving it in a lavatory cupboard. Local dissident nationals have already helped in a similar manner to effect the death of passengers on skyjacked planes. After all, if in twenty years the U.S. security services never suspected the spy that damaged the country most in its two-hundred-year history (John Walker), can you blame airline X that it didn't know of all of the affiliations of that attractive reservations clerk whose current boyfriend happened to be a member of Abu Nidal's hit squad and asked her to do a small favor by putting his heavy suitcase

on the conveyer belt to save him overweight charges on a
flight that he, as it happened, didn't take?

JUSTIFIABLY WE THINK of the plane's crew as the friends
and guardians of the passengers. The cockpit crew are the
people on whose cool professionalism one relies for getting
to one's destination safely.

Almost all pilots and many crew members of hijacked
airplanes have been models of exemplary conduct both
during the initial hijacking and afterward. But one major
airline disaster of 1985 was at first suspected to have been
caused by a member of the flight deck crew having taken
aboard "as a favor for a friend" a parcel that exploded in
mid-air and killed all aboard. Shouldn't members of the
crew and their hand baggage go through the metal detector and a frisking each time they board, or is the Airline
Pilots' Union or the strong flight attendant union going to
balk?

WHILE AIRPORT SECURITY procedures have not piled up a
terrific record for catching terrorists before they board, at
one of the most secure airports in the world, that at
Frankfurt-am-Main in Germany, security measures
caught one *counter*terrorist, namely me.

I had just completed a nondangerous assignment of
demonstrating to a certain West German counterterrorist
organization some advanced radio equipment for remote
detonation of a more sophisticated type than that already
in use by some terrorist groups in other countries. I was
dropped off at the airport a bit late, quickly checked my
bag to Heathrow in London, and hurried to make a necessary phone call to England. I was advised that I had to
stay an extra day in Germany!

I must explain that one of the earlier security procedures
at Frankfurt was that when you checked in, a red self-stick
dot was put on your ticket and a green dot was put on your
bag. If you checked in more than one bag, your red dot

would have on it the number of bags you checked. The captain of the plane himself checked before takeoff to see that the number of red dots corresponded to the number of green dots used, counting the multiple bags designated on the red dots.

I went to the check-in counter, explained that I would not be flying that day, and wanted to arrange for a flight the following day. I didn't want to cause trouble and was quite prepared to have my already checked-in bag held at Heathrow for my arrival the following day. I had the necessities for a layover in my hand-carried luggage.

But the captain had already decided against takeoff because the numbers on the red and green stickers didn't correspond and there was an unaccompanied bag—the one great danger everyone was on the lookout for!

Needless to say, I caused a great inconvenience that day. My bag had to be found and unloaded. I was told to go down to a certain part of the baggage collection area and wait for my bag to appear on the belt.

The baggage area I was sent to was conspicuously empty of people. Though I was alone, I was sure I was being discreetly observed through a two-way mirror. Was I going to claim the bag when it came down the chute, or was I going to leave it and take off?

Of course when the bag came down, I took it and quickly took it to customs through the "Nothing to Declare" portal. I was immediately apprehended by the police and made to open my bag as they watched. Inside was remote detonation radio equipment!

I explained my role as a demonstrator of the equipment, but they decided not to believe me. I was held for a period of four hours until finally my request to see a senior official was granted. I gave him what I was most reluctant to give the customs officers and police—the phone number of a senior GSG9 counterterrorist officer, who, when called, had to come from Wiesbaden to the Frankfurt airport to identify both himself and me personally, to my considerable embarrassment since I normally go to great lengths to maintain a low profile when traveling.

I completed my extra day's work, then flew off to Heathrow with my bag and a new appreciation of the security system at Frankfurt. It was efficient and low key. Alertness overruled the complacency present at many other airports.

The existence of a force such as the GSG9 border guard, dedicated to the roll of counterterrorism, obviously pays dividends. The tried and simple method of flightdeck crew confirming a passenger/baggage count also worked. In this case, a vigilant British Airways captain rightly decided not to move until the rogue bag was removed despite pressure from various parts of the system to get off the stand and stay on schedule. The fatalistic shrug-of-the-shoulders acceptance that terrorism is here to stay has diminished this conscientious attitude of air crews as demonstrated by the double Air India disaster.

MOST HIJACKERS TODAY belong to militant Arab groups. You would think that one of their major targets would be El Al flights. The case is otherwise. The only time an El Al flight was successfully skyjacked was back in 1968, when PLO members took over an El Al flight and forced it to land in Algeria. Nobody got hurt. A couple of years later, an Arab man and woman tried to hijack an El Al plane flying from Amsterdam to New York. There were two Israeli sky marshals aboard. While a single sky marshal is usually ineffective against an attempted hijack, these Israeli security men killed the male hijacker and captured the woman. The plane landed safely in London, and no El Al plane has been hijacked since.

The Israelis also take extreme security measures to avoid hijackings, and the Arab terrorists know it. Their baggage inspection is thorough. Every piece going aboard in the cargo compartment is examined for bombs. The cargo compartments themselves are reinforced with armor plating. This precaution worked well in August of 1972 when a bomb went off in an El Al 707 that had left Rome with 140 passengers and eight crew members aboard. The bomb exploded when air pressure inside the baggage hold decreased (baggage holds, unlike passenger compartments, are not pressurized), but the damage was apparently limited to a six-inch hole and a smallish crack in the rear door. The 707 was able to return safely to Rome with no one hurt.

Now the Israelis go a step further. After a thorough initial search, bags and other cargo are placed inside armored altitude chambers. The air is then pumped out of these armored casings, simulating the decrease in atmosphere pressure in the baggage hold as the aircraft goes higher. If any bag contained an explosive that relied on air pressure rather than time delay, it would go off harmlessly in the armored container.

The security staffs of El Al also conduct passenger interrogations of a depth not characteristic of any other airline. Even Americans boarding flights at John F. Kennedy International Airport in New York bound for Israel have ground checks made to ascertain they are who they say they are before they can board. Passengers are usually asked to arrive two and a half hours before flight time to allow sufficient time for the baggage security procedures and the questioning. They are asked whether they did their own packing; whether they were carrying any electronic devices and if so where they were bought; whether they were carrying anything given to them by somebody else; whether any other person had access to their luggage after it was packed at any time. And answers, if the security men have any suspicions, are cross-checked by telephone with family or friends of passengers.

True, this takes time, and must be viewed by some passengers as a nuisance, just as others favor these procedures as extra precautions that seemed to have helped make El Al safe from hijacking for a decade.

Most such passengers are unaware that, even when they are in flight, they are protected by devices under the wings of El Al planes that can alter the flight of any surface-to-air missile that a terrorist might launch as the plane was taking off or landing.

It must be added that El Al in this case luxuriates in not being a high-volume airline like the big American, British, and some European carriers, for whom taking these security measures is unfeasible. If every airline employed them, there would quickly come a point of diminishing returns. As is, airport check-in routine and waiting time and then additional waiting time for baggage can take longer than some flights do.

I DO NOT want to give anyone the impression that flying is dangerous. Surely many more people have been hurt, robbed, or killed by muggers than have been hurt or killed in all hijackings everywhere. The point I am driving at is that the statistical possibility of any individual air traveler being on a hijacked plane is remote, but false comfort should not be taken from the incomplete measures now taken on the ground to try to prevent hijackers from smuggling weapons aboard. It is therefore indispensable for passengers to know what to do to minimize their chances of being hurt during a skyjacking. And it is equally indispensable to have a rapid reaction team respond to a skyjacking in a way that will diminish the number of skyjackings over time because terrorists will begin to see that the chances of achieving their objectives are poor; that the chances of their being killed or apprehended have increased; and that the terrorist "sport" of skyjacking no longer creates the kind of media attention that is its psychological fuel and political objective.

IN A SKYJACKING, the first aim of the terrorists is to cause panic among the passengers in order for a few people (the terrorists) to be able to exercise absolute control over a large number of people (passengers and crew) in a confined space. While waiting to make their move, the hijackers have been building up to an emotional peak. At the moment that they announce the hijack, they will usually make a lot of noise, show their weapons, and try to create an appearance of chaos that only they can control. Submerging people in chaos guarantees the freezing of their reactions. The terrorists want to create the maximum amount of anxiety—fear of the unknown—in the minimum amount of time. The result is control by fear.

It is at the beginning of a flight that the hijackers are most primed. They are at their emotional peak. They must make their move soon in order to take advantage of a fully fueled aircraft that increases their alternatives for diverting and rediverting the plane if that becomes necessary as landing rights are refused.

At the same time that the terrorists are at their emotional peak, the passengers are relaxed, glad to be on their way. Thus the terrorists and the passengers are at opposite ends of their emotional cycle, one peaking, one relaxing. That makes it so much easier to create the panic that leads to control.

However, it is important to remember that the terrorists' adrenaline high incorporates their fear, and that is what leads to the sacrificial first killing of a passenger. They have been instructed to avoid overkill. But they are encouraged by their mentors to make the sacrificial killing brutal in order to derive the maximum benefit from the act. Nobody wants to be killed. Nobody wants to be killed *like that*. A planeload of normal human beings, frightened as never before in their lives, is transformed into a fuselage full of sheep ready to do the terrorists' bidding.

How then should a passenger behave if he happens to find himself on a plane that is hijacked? My first advice is: *Don't try to be a hero*. The stewards and stewardesses aboard have been trained to help avoid panic among passengers, as they would in a nonhijacking mishap, and to minimize the danger to life. They do have a minor amount of training in what to do when skyjacked, but they are not trained as counterterrorists. Even those of us who have been so taught would have a hard time of it if we were passengers on a hijacked flight. The initial reaction should be to suppress the will to fight and blend in with the background as a passenger.

One of the most publicized skyjackings of the decade took place in 1985, when TWA Flight 847 out of Athens was taken over by two hijackers. That was a classic case of terrorist cost effectiveness that resulted in riveting public attention for weeks on the terrorists' objectives and converting some of the hostages into complacent handmaidens of the terrorists.

This skyjacking proved to be, in terms of media exposure, one of the most successful of all time. Yet it started out badly for the terrorists.

Only two of the three terrorists who were meant to get aboard did so. (The third, who was arrested by the Greeks, was allowed to leave Greece almost immediately after his arrest. This may not have been just stupidity. Greek police authorities have been infiltrated at a high level by terrorist sympathizers and actual Soviet GRU operatives. In 1985 two senior police officials were arrested for espionage.)

The two terrorists who got aboard did not have weapons with them. The weapons—handguns, hand grenades, and Mace cannisters—were already aboard Flight 847, hidden in a rear toilet by helpful hands on the ground. Even so, the terrorists found only one of the guns.

The first indication that a hijack was in progress came when the two terrorists ran down the aisle toward the front of the plane, shouting and spraying Mace (a gas that temporarily disables people by blinding and choking them, like tear gas) over the tops of the seats.

The lead hijacker demanded the key to the flight deck from the chief air hostess, Uli Derickson, who bravely claimed not to have it. Another hostess had just enough time to grab the intercom phone and transmit the emergency hijack signal to the pilot before the hijacker kicked open the door to the flight deck. At this point all the people in the passenger area of the Boeing 727 were choking, their eyes streaming from the effects of the Mace. Let us now envision a scenario.

Suppose that I, a highly trained counterterrorist, was on that flight. Could I have aborted the skyjacking or caused it to conclude differently?

If I'd had a window seat, that would have been a problem. I usually try for an aisle seat, but knowledgeable hijackers rearrange the passengers to put able-bodied males in window seats. Suppose that I had a weapon with me or that I was the person who had found the 9-mm Browning automatic that the hijackers had overlooked in the toilet. (The male passenger who did in fact find it *gave it to the hijackers*. At the minimum, he could have left the gun where it was, or he could have reconcealed it or dropped it into the used towel compartment. If he had the barest knowledge about handguns, he could have separated the bullet-holding magazine from the gun and emptied it of bullets before reinserting the magazine into the handgrip of the gun. He did not assist in his chances of survival by simply handing the missing gun over to his captors.)

Assuming I did have a weapon, would it have made sense for me to have a go at the terrorists once the Mace had cleared? The first danger to me could have come from another passenger, who, seeing that I had a gun, might try to restrain me if he mistook me for a terrorist. Or, more likely, he would have thought me to be a civilian like himself and have been afraid that any action I might take would fail since he would have no foreknowledge of my specialist training. He might fear the consequences of my action and be right to do so.

Now, let's deal with the fact that terrorists like to use hand grenades precisely because they can do more damage to more people, especially in the crowded confines of a plane, than bullets from a pistol. Because a grenade bursts in all directions, it is a terrifying weapon in itself once the safety pin holding the handle in place has been removed. When the pin is pulled (it usually has a large circular end to make removal easier), the only thing that keeps the grenade from going off is the grenade user's fingers on the lever that had been held in place by the pin. Once the lever, which is on a spring mechanism, is released, you have passed the point of no return. A timer takes over and, in no more than four seconds, the grenade will explode. That provides just enough time for the user to throw the grenade and seek cover for himself. But the terrorist on the plane has already committed his life to the venture. If he is going to be killed, he will want to take as many others with him as possible.

If a terrorist in a plane is holding a grenade from which the pin has been removed (which he would usually do only if he intended to detonate it) and a gun in his other hand, even with my close-quarter combat training I'd have a real problem. I couldn't shoot him from a distance because his grenade hand would open, the lever would spring open automatically, and the grenade would go off. That means I would have to get close enough to grab the grenade hand *first* to keep it from opening and then shoot him. Thus my training to SAS standards to hit a three-inch target two times in three seconds even if the target is holding a living hostage in front of him *would do no good*. And while I was getting close enough to grab the grenade hand, I'd be a target for the terrorist. I'd have to be damn lucky to get close to the terrorist without his sensing danger from me, grab his grenade hand, shoot him, and keep holding his hand with the grenade and take a head shot at the other terrorist, who might be at the other end of the plane and too far to hit with a handgun. And I would still have to deal with the pinless grenade!

Even if I was successful, the immediate result would be panic on the plane because the passengers wouldn't know what was going on. I would have to take verbal control, even threaten to shoot anyone who moved, in order to achieve a stunned silence.

There is one added danger. While most hijackers reveal themselves immediately, really smart ones might keep one of their number unacknowledged, watching out for the reaction of the sky marshal, if there was one. If there was a third terrorist, he'd probably have assumed I was a sky marshal and the only obstacle he'd have to face was me. I would be shouting for one of the crew members to get the captain, so I could pass control to him, but in that period I would be vulnerable to the third hijacker, or the second if he was too far back for me to have shot him. Most likely, I might have been shot by the first hijacker before I got to his grenade hand.

You can see the difficulties in that scenario, even for a trained operative, which is why sky marshals, who receive far less training than I've had and have had far less experience with terrorists, are pretty ineffective. If a terrorist suspects there is a sky marshal aboard, he will simply ask the people in the first row to stand up and say, "Would the sky marshal please identify himself or these three people will be killed at once." What option would the sky marshal have? And if the terrorists' suspicions were wrong, people would be needlessly killed as the terrorists tried to get a nonexistent marshal to reveal himself.

If I or a sky marshal would be ineffective under the circumstances, the ordinary passenger should never attempt to be a hero. If you are ever caught in a hijacking, I would urge you to observe the following recommendations:

1. Do not look a terrorist in the eye. Terrorists may interpret eye contact as resistance and pick you for a ritual sacrifice.

2. Do not be belligerent in anything you say or do. For

instance, if you are a large man, keep in mind that many terrorists are small in stature and the mere act of your standing up unexpectedly might seem a threat to them.

3. Don't try to intimidate a terrorist. Some people when stopped by a police car will allude to "pull" or influence they have or how important they or a relative are. Don't ever try that on a terrorist because the more "important" you are the better you serve their purposes as a potential victim. On the contrary, try to be as inconspicuous as possible. Don't ask questions of the hijackers. If the hijackers speak to you, keep neutral; don't try to patronize them by pretending to be on their side politically; at the same time, don't say anything against them or their cause. If asked for your opinion, try, if feasible, to say you don't know enough about the subject to comment. Some hijackers like to spout off about their cause. Pay attention to them while they are talking, but don't volunteer an opinion about anything if possible. Be polite, but try not to be subservient.

4. Hijackers are near-paranoid in their suspicions, so try to avoid conversation, even whispered conversation, with other passengers. It is extremely dangerous to confide in another passenger, however friendly they may seem. When exposed to danger, another passenger may trade your confidence in the usually false expectation that he will be treated well for ratting on you. Some people behave marvelously in emergencies, but others quickly become rats and stool pigeons. Arab hijackers have been known to collect passports both as a means of control and to single out passengers with Jewish-sounding names. They frequently guess wrong. Remember that Muslim Arabs (Christian Arabs have not been known to hijack airplanes) despise Jews but hate their Christian Arab adversaries also. They also hate Americans, but some have particular hatreds for European nations that have taken terrorists prisoner. Don't try to second-guess whether the hijackers will "like" you. Be as neutral as possible.

5. Some hijackers rob passengers of their valuables. Don't try to hide anything. If you value your life, turn over to them whatever they are asking for. Don't plead to retain something for "sentimental" reasons. They'll take it anyway, and you'll only have made yourself conspicuous.

6. Always ask permission of one of the hijackers before getting up, changing your seat, or going to the lavatory. If they refuse permission, it may be because they do not understand you. If someone does not translate for you, keep calm, and try again later with another of the hijackers. It is good practice to use the bathroom facilities in the airport before any flight because hijackings usually take place in the first part of a flight. You are least likely to be permitted to use the lavatory shortly after the hijacking when the terrorists are seeking to insure control over the passengers. Minimize your intake of coffee, tea, water, or other beverages to avoid unnecessary trips to the bathroom. Never forget that rising fear has an effect on the bladder. In the unlikely event that the hijackers offer you an alcoholic beverage, accept it but avoid drinking it. You will want to have 100 percent of your wits about you all the time even though you are trying to be passive and inconspicuous.

7. Take guidance from the flight or cabin crew. While they have not been trained in hostage rescue operations, most airline crews have received instructions on procedures to be followed during a hijack. Some of the things they may be doing may not make sense to you but could be part of their instructions that are designed to aid in a rescue later. Their responsibilities are enormous while they, too, have to overcome their fears and rely on training and common sense. They are often a mediating influence on the terrorists who, despite everything, need to communicate with whoever is controlling them on the ground. Put your faith in your flight crew's judgment.

8. It is important that you *think* correctly instead of lending yourself to panic. You should know that once the

terrorists achieve control over the body of the people on the plane, *nothing happens immediately.* Your most frightening enemy can be time. Therefore think *days* instead of *hours.* Remind yourself that you and your fellow passengers are not alone. By that time, millions of people around the world are with you, hoping for your relief.

9. If relief comes in the form of a rescue by a rapid response team on the ground, the moment you sense this is happening get down between the horizontal rows of seats and stay there. Do not let your feet get into the aisle. Do not sit or stand up until ordered to do so *by the assault team.*

I HAVE BEEN asked are there ways of avoiding getting on a plane that will be hijacked. If there were a foolproof way, it would be an instant solution to the hijack problem, for everyone would avoid planes that might be hijacked. I have heard people being advised to book on airlines of neutral nations, but they forget that even a Swiss aircraft has been blown out of the sky by terrorists. There is no neutrality from terrorism. Perhaps the one thing that would help if you are traveling on holiday is to avoid airports that have been tempting to hijackers frequently, such as Athens. And if you are traveling on business, you might try to avoid stopovers in such places, even if you don't intend to get off the plane.

There are some precautions that can be taken both before your trip and at the airport.

1. Make a note of your passport number, date of issue, and place where it was issued, and put this information some place other than a wallet or handbag since these might be taken from you. This information will assist your identification after the hijacking is over.

2. If you have ever traveled to Israel and your passport has been marked with an entrance or exit stamp, you may want to take the precaution of getting a new passport. The Israelis, incidentally, will avoid stamping your passport if you ask. U.S. passports and those of some other countries

have a place to fill in the name and address of the person you want notified in an emergency. *This information could be useful to a hijacker.* Some immigration authorities routinely photocopy this information. There is no legal obligation for you to have this information in your passport. If you are renewing yours, you might to omit this information and simply carry emergency information elsewhere on your person.

3. Most travel agents will supply you with a typed itinerary. If you leave a copy with a member of your family or friend, be certain to advise them not to release this information to anybody unless they are sure the information won't fall into the wrong hands. do not keep your itinerary with your plane tickets if there is some destination on it that might give a hijacker the wrong idea.

4. Don't put medicines or anything else necessary to your health in your checked baggage. Keep them with you in your carry-on bag or pocket of your coat. Keep prescriptions in the original bottle to avoid wrong-guessing by others.

5. Most Muslims react adversely to your carrying alcohol or skin magazines. Leave such magazines at home, and if traveling a high-risk route, you might want to skip the duty-free liquor concession.

6. If you belong to a veterans' organization or any political organization that might be considered controversial by terrorists, leave your organization ID cards at home. If you work in defense industries or the military, you might want to carry anything that would identify you as such in your checked luggage rather than your wallet or carry-on bag. Military personel should travel in civilian clothes whenever permitted. This is especially true for U.S. military personnel, who are easy selections for the ritual killing that so many hijackers now require to prove that they are serious.

7. I have strong feelings about everyone being entitled to read whatever they want to, but I must caution you that

when you fly you might not want to have with you literature that is anti-Communist, religious, or might be con-
strued to have an Israeli or political connection.

8. For traveling most people choose comfortable, loose-
fitting clothing. That's fine, but also use another criterion.
You don't want your clothing to make you conspicuous.

9. With the number of vicious attacks that have taken
place against civilians in airports, there are some obvious
precautions I would now recommend. You don't want to
hang around an airport unnecessarily; so check with the
airline before you leave home to make sure the plane is still
scheduled to depart on time. If curbside luggage check-in is
available, use it so that you don't have to line up at a ticket
counter unnecessarily or for a long time. Don't hang
around exposed public areas. If you have to wait near the
gate area, stay away from large glass windows, and face
away from such windows. If you have a choice of seats in a
waiting room, don't sit next to a wastepaper repository or
near any luggage that doesn't seem to belong to someone.
A phone booth should be looked into before entering; if
there's a package in there, notify airport security.

10. In the unlikely but possible case that you hear a
bomb warning given, follow the instructions immediately.
If no instructions are given, get down flat on the floor. And
do that immediately if you hear gunfire or explosions
anywhere nearby. Do not scatter and run in panic. Bullets
will win every time.

THE READER MIGHT very well be thinking at this point *Who
wants to live this way?* Who wants to have to take all these
complex precautions for a business or pleasure trip, especially for the latter? Who wants to have to worry about
these things, or hide one's identity, or examine a book or a
magazine as if one was a censor? And what about taking
children on trips fraught with hazard?

The answer is nobody wants to live that way, and that is
exactly how terrorists create a climate of fear that works to

their advantage. That is why the orientation of this book is toward the elimination of terrorists, which would in itself get rid of the other concerns.

WE NOW TURN to an example of a badly handled hijacking, that of TWA Flight 847 out of Athens on June 14, 1985. That capture of a Boeing 727 turned into a triumph for the hijackers. It could have been handled differently by highly trained professionals.

Robert Stetham of Waldorf, Maryland, would be alive today if the hijacking of TWA 847 had been handled properly. There would have been no days of anguish for the passengers and their families while Nabih Berri pretended to play good-guy mediator between the "bad" hijackers and the world that wanted the hostages freed. It was on the second landing of 847 in Beirut that twelve more terrorists boarded the aircraft, making an assault next to impossible. These twelve bravos, having hijacked nothing, acted like barbarians, shouting, screaming, and stealing whatever they could from the terrified passengers. Meanwhile, Berri's TV drama got him exactly what he wanted, instant worldwide fame, and the hijackers got what they wanted, a media event that lasted for seventeen days, with millions of air travelers feeling how helpless they would be in the shoes of the hostages.

There needn't have been any helplessness because help was at hand as close as the U.S. military installation near Frankfurt. It was said at the time that the United States just couldn't get a Delta team from South Carolina to the Middle East fast enough. It didn't have to. There was a Delta team in Europe, a relatively short flight away from Algiers, the first place that the hijacked plane was permitted to land that was suitable for an assault. The plane was on the ground there for ten hours, much more than a rapid response team requires for a successful assault. Moreover, there were certain advantages in the fact that TWA's five stewardesses were all in or near their forties, mature per-

sons who, on evidence, helped the survival of the passengers. The chief stewardess, Uli Derickson, was a real
heroine, not only for risking her life by refusing to help the
hijackers sort out passports to identify Americans and
Jews, but when the chief terrorist was ready to go bananas
because money was demanded for refueling the plane, she
calmed the situation by paying the fuel bill on her credit
card. She is a tribute to her profession.

THE FACT THAT TWA 847 had been hijacked was known
minutes after the aircraft took off from Athens. Because
the plane belonged to an American airline, it was the
prerogative of the United States to have its special forces
conduct the assault, but had Delta asked for SAS help as
the German GSG9 did for the Mogadishu attack, it would
have been forthcoming at once.

One must remember that the Delta team is committed to
an assault, not to negotiation. It should never be used
when negotiation is a viable alternative, but the student of
hijackings will know that negotiation gives the terrorists
what they want (publicity and the creation of fear) and
opens the way to future hijackings. It would be the prerogative of the government to obtain swift permission from
the Algerian government for its assault team to land.
There was no established international mechanism to
bring this about in sufficient time.

Time permitting, the rapid response team would have
landed before the hijacked airplane. Failing that, they
could have chosen to land in a plane that might have
seemed part of normal commercial traffic—if such flights
were continued after the hijacked plane landed—or, preferably, they would have used HALO, high altitude, low
opening parachute drops in which all such assault teams
are highly trained. Basically, this involves leaving the
plane at 25,000 feet—too high to be heard or observed by
the hijackers—and free-falling to a predetermined 3,500 to
1,500 feet from the ground before opening parachutes. We

New Zealanders are particularly expert in this kind of free-fall with full equipment, and our expertise is readily on call, along with other SAS and special forces detachments.

The area around the hijacked plane must by prearrangement be sealed off and other law enforcement people kept away. One section of the assault team sets up a surveillance group. A second group takes its position around the perimeter, armed with night-vision light-enhancing surveillance scopes attached to 7.62-caliber sniper rifles. The third part is the actual assault group that will enter the plane.

The surveillance team, one or two at a time, with practiced precision, will make a concealed approach to the plane under cover of darkness and from the rear, which is the blind spot for people aboard, including the terrorists. Their concealment must be total in case the terrorist group has eyes on the outside supporting their actions and communicating with them by light signal or other coded means. One of the tasks the surveillance people are trained for is to drill holes in the skin of the aircraft in order to insert surreptitiously the means of both hearing what is going on inside the plane and actually seeing what is happening inside. These men are trained in the use of very high speed drills in a manner that is very nearly noiseless (sometimes diversions are needed to cover up the noise). These men have also perfected the handling of the drills on exactly the same aircraft bodies so that they will know the moment they have pierced the aluminum skin of the plane and stop at once.

The surveillance experts have several ways of getting their holes drilled into the cabin, depending on the type of aircraft. They can come in from the outside near the rear toilets (but not into the toilet compartments, because the closed doors would prevent seeing what was going on in the passenger compartment) or drill into the cabin from inside the baggage compartment or nose wheel compartment. They will then implant miniature mikes, which are

tiny eavesdropping bugs attached to velcro and placed in
the carpeting under the passenger seats in a manner that
will enable the bugs to pick up sound at preplanned locations throughout the aircraft. Monitoring movements all
along the fuselage of the plane is made possible by laying
strip mikes along the inner skin of the fuselage.

For the cockpit they use a very sophisticated but classic
bug on a tiny rubber suction device that is attached by a
long cane rod from underneath to the plexiglass of an odd
corner of the windshield, thus enabling sound from inside
the cockpit to be picked up by a laser unit at some distance.

At this point, the surveillance team is able to hear
sounds from within all parts of the aircraft. This makes it
possible for them to pinpoint the movements of the
hijackers. They identify sounds and continue to monitor
them up until the last moments before the assault.

One of the more interesting counterterrorist develop-
ments of recent years is the fiber optic lens that is much
like a fly's eye and can "see" in a multitude of directions.
The appropriate lens is chosen for the required field of
vision. This triumph of miniaturized technology is in-
serted into a drilled hole in the aircraft at the end of a thin
probe The "eye" is placed where, undetected, it will have
as clear as possible a vision of movement within the fuselage of the plane, which is transmitted to a remote video
monitor.

Thus through sight and sound, the surveillance group
can identify the hijackers and keep track of their movements. They are passing on information to the actual
assault group, which would normally be at least five men,
perhaps a few more if the plane is a wide-bodied type, such
as the Air Bus, Lockheed L-1011, McDonnell Douglas DC
10 or new Boeing 757/767 series. The even larger Boeing
747 series, with their many partitions and spread passenger loads, demands that larger teams be used to cover
the simultaneous multiple entry required to ensure the safe
neutralization of the whole aircraft. The 747, one of the
most common types on international flights, presents a

further special situation because it has a second floor, an upstairs lounge (sometimes used for extra seating) for first class passengers and the flight crew compartment. There is a safety exit on this upper floor with an approach along the fuselage. That would be used by the assault team as an additional entrance. One member of the upper deck assault team would have been assigned immediately after the entry to secure the bottom of the staircase. The remainder would secure the cockpit. The coordination and timing of such an assault are crucial and so are rehearsed over and over again.

The use of too many men is stupid and dangerous if uncoordinated. The worst recent example is that of the Egyptian commandos who used far too large an assault force in their attempt to rescue the hostages on an Egyptair 737, which is a small plane. That entire operation was ill conceived. It wasn't rehearsed the way a trained response team would be. The American observers on the spot had an intimidating effect on the Egyptians, who were concerned about face-saving. They should have left the task to properly trained professionals. Instead they stormed the plane with a crowd, and the fiasco ended with the death of many hostages.

A properly trained assault team has a plastic layout of the particular aircraft, and with the use of flow pencils, approaches are studied. If time permits, they will rehearse on a duplicate aircraft. They need to know whether the hijackers have placed explosives against the fuselage of the plane. Such explosives will normally have detonating wires going in one direction to the place from which they can be set off. The surveillance group identifies both the layout of the explosive devices and, just before the assault, the position of the terrorist who, by his actions or words, will seem to be the one charged with detonating the explosives. Heading off such a detonation by shooting the would-be detonator becomes a high priority for one of the assault team members first entering the plane.

The rescuers also need to know if the passengers are

hysterical or calm. One of the reasons for staging assaults in the middle of the night or toward morning is that the passengers and hijackers alike are at their low ebb. But since it is wise to stage the assault as quickly as possible— and there may be good reasons for not waiting till night-fall, particularly if the hijackers are demanding to move elsewhere at once—a daylight assault may be necessary. Negotiations will be used to avoid this.

Throughout, communication is maintained with the cockpit crew to learn of the hijackers' demands, the need for food, et cetera, but also to use such conversations as a means of luring the terrorist leader into the cockpit for a "communication" just before the assault, particularly if in daylight. If he is out of sight of the other terrorists, they will be looking for him when the assault starts and thus be momentarily distracted. Ideally, when the terrorist leader is lured into the cockpit to talk to his outside link, things are said to him to get him excited and issuing angry threats. This, too, is unsettling to the other terrorists, who may hear him shouting but not know what he is shouting about. Psychology is a major factor in the assault plan.

For the assault, the team members wear balaclavas, showing only their eyes and mouth. They also present a fearsome spectacle to the terrorists, as they did when the SAS liberated the Iranian Embassy in London. When seconds count, it all matters. They are dressed either all in black or in dark camouflage outfits. Each man is equipped with a 9-mm Browning pistol (or sometimes a Sig-Sauer or Walther PPK) with low velocity ammunition, ideally suited for firing in a confined space without loss of accu-racy but with minimum danger of exiting from a terrorist's head or body and wounding and killing a passenger. Some will use the Heckler and Koch MP 5 submachine gun, if called for.

As soon as the entry point or points are selected, the assault team members get their individual assignments. If the TWA 847 plane had been taken in Algiers, it is likely that the assault team would have decided to go through two or more doors simultaneously. A frame charge made of Dartcord-type flexible lead-cased shaped explosive would be used. The power of this kind of charge can be varied when used as a framed charge. It will have been tested on a model of a replica of the plane being assaulted. It is applied to the outside of each door with ordinary masking tape. A ten-second fuse is attached to the detonator. The charge is designed to fracture the frame of the door, blowing it inwards but not across the fuselage where it could harm passengers. Actually, one man's weight against the blown door will push it in. It is vital that the door is severed cleanly to prevent distortion by the explosive jamming the hinges. The explosion is a controlled one and rapid entry is then essential. The first man in throws himself immediately down on the door, and the leapfrogging begins. The next man in is the stun grenade expert. This grenade creates a lot of noise and dust and smoke and smell in the darkened plane. Earlier model stun grenades give off one bright blinding flash and several seconds of noise that pounds the inner ear. The newer stun grenades can give off up to eight reports and eight flashes in one and a half to two seconds and can be far more effective in some situations.

The stun grenade is hurled in a predetermined direction based on the intelligence from the surveillance group. Naturally, the intention is for all the hijackers to be temporarily blinded and deafened by the stun grenades. The grenade hurler will then fall flat so that the rest of the assault team can literally run right over his back. These men will have flashlights fitted to their 9-mm weapons. Each will have a 30°-40° "slice of the pie," a portion of the plane in which any hijacker is his target. One man will have been assigned to head straight for the cockpit to shoot the terrorist leader. All of these men, as I have already described, are trained to fire killing shots in rapid succession. They also promote noise by shouting *"Stay down! Stay down!"* at the passengers, who are best off cowering in front of their seats and not getting in the way of anyone's line of fire.

The men who come crashing into your plane are experts. They have rehearsed the assault dozens of times to get their timing down to half seconds. When they go in, they go in for the kill. There is no margin for error or hesitation at this point. I have experience of such assaults, and the violence is sudden, rapid, and extremely final. You are dedicated to your target being dead seconds after you enter. In reality, it takes just a fraction longer. This is an efficient violence that you, as a member of the public, have never witnessed before—and will never want to witness again. It is difficult for a layman to comprehend such precision under such duress. It exists, it is trained for, and it is on your side. During preparation for the assault, all the ifs, buts, and what ifs are coldly and professionally talked through and accommodated in the plan. The objective is—*kill the terrorists before they kill again.* The public should be aware of such a capability and have confidence in its execution.

An important part of the surveillance has been to determine if there is a so-called sleeping terrorist, that is, a terrorist who may not be one of those who ran up and down the aisles terrifying the passengers. If it is known that there is such a man, one of the assault team will have him as a target. Even after the immediate assault, the team members will be on the lookout for anyone among the passengers who is not really a passenger. "Sleeping" terrorists are rare but are a factor to be considered.

Once the terrorists have been hit, the assault team gets out as quickly as it entered. The passengers are left to local law enforcement and airline people. By the time the media gets a good look at the exiting hostages, the assault team should have vanished into the night, their rescue over.

Remember that of the three original hijackers, only two succeeded in getting aboard TWA 847 undetected. A five-man assault team would surely have had the situation under control in seconds.

Would it have been worth doing? And doing it while the plane was on the ground in Algiers? Robert Stethem was killed as a demonstration only after TWA 847 landed in Beirut the second time and the so-called militants went aboard, reinforcing the original two hijackers.

Perhaps if you are uncertain about whether it would have been worth doing, ask Robert Stethem's parents.

5

Networking

A new and for me nasty word has come into the English language. It is so new, I gather, that it does not even appear in the most recent dictionary. The word is "networking," and it is being used to mean using friends or "contacts" (people one has met, or friends of friends) to further one's aspirations, business goals, or getting a job. For those of us in counterterrorist work, the word has more sinister connotations, for in the last two decades or so, networking has accelerated so among terrorist groups that one is forced to think of terrorism as a universal plague in which the wanton killers of all nationalities have linked arms against their common enemy: the rest of us.

ITEM: IN APRIL of 1985, a Palestinian terrorist named Ali Minour fired a bazooka at the Jordanian embassy in Rome, presumably because King Hussein was working toward a peace process for the ravaged Middle East. Minour was caught and questioned. Finally, he cracked, and revealed that he got the bazooka from a woman he believed to be either *Italian* or *French*.

Item: The Brazilian Popular Revolutionary Vanguard
(VPR), after murdering a British sailor in a Brazilian port,
issued a statement: "This is an expression of solidarity
with the combatants of Ireland and all the world."

Item: In September of 1985, a sixteen-year-old terrorist
(the age is increasingly typical) named Hassan Aatab
threw a bomb into the British Airways office in Rome, on
the Via Veneto in the heart of the city. Aatab was caught
and questioned. He revealed that the bomb was given to
him by a tall, blond man he knew only as "the *Belgian.*"

Item: Three North Korean women in their early twenties, trained as snipers, in 1983 were sent on loan to Khomeini in Iran to infiltrate Iraq and assassinate certain
designated field grade Iraqi officers. It's hard to imagine
why North Korean women were chosen for the mission.
True, they were expert at picking off targets at a distance.
But women are notably conspicuous in northern Iraq, and
Oriental women would be most conspicuous. Perhaps it
was intended that they do their job, be caught and, close-
mouthed, die, leaving Iran out of the picture and the Iraqis
confused and perhaps even humiliated because death at
the hands of women in the male chauvinist Arab world
guarantees a loss of face few Westerners can appreciate.

The three North Korean women managed to kill a dozen
Iraqis before they were caught. The Iraqis are rather inexperienced in interrogating Orientals. Arab fierceness met
a stone wall of resistance and silence. I was in Baghdad at
the time and was coopted to attend the interrogations. A
frustrated Iraqi colonel thought a more sympathetic foreign face might work. It did. I was the only white Anglo-
Saxon in the room, and I had to work through an inter-
preter, but my technique was basically humane under the
circumstances, and particularly in sharp contrast to the
earlier interrogations. I didn't have complete success. Only
one of the women broke down, but that proved to be
enough. I learned how they were infiltrated into Iraq, what
their instructions were, which Iranian group ran them

(ran in the sense that a control runs a spy), and, most important, information about another group also trained by the North Koreans for similar mischief.

The information extracted from this North Korean terrorist was of value not only to the Iraqis but to the Western counterterrorists with whom I am in contact. With this information in hand, the Iraqis executed the three women.

If the reader finds their executions ruthless, it should be remembered that these three had volunteered to murder ranking Iraqi officers and had in fact killed a dozen before they were apprehended. The murders—like all terrorist murders—were premeditated. Had the women been tried, convicted, and jailed, that would merely have been the incitement for another terrorist act in which hostages would be killed—or exchanged for the women. The hostages need not be Iraqis. If they were Americans, the United States would find itself putting pressure on Iraq behind the scenes, and the cycle would have escalated once again.

Sometimes the North Korean terrorists range closer to home, if you can think of Burma, nearly two thousand miles from Korea, as close. A couple of years before the incident described above, a group of South Korean dignitaries, including the leader of the Cabinet, were visiting Rangoon on a diplomatic mission. The platform on which they stood to pay verbal homage to their hosts exploded, killing a number of leading South Korean politicians. Three of the assassins were captured. They were, of course, North Koreans, operating not as soldiers but as terrorists, long after the official war between North and South Korea had ended.

None of this should be surprising if one remembers the first Arab-Japanese terrorist link-up. The Lod Massacre took place on May 31, 1972. Three Japanese "tourists" (actually members of the Japanese Red Army coopted by Wadi Hadad's PFLP) machine-gunned over one hundred Christian pilgrims at Israel's main airport, using weapons previously infiltrated. Kozo Okomoto, one of the three

Japanese, survived the killing of twenty-six and the wounding of seventy-six. He was sentenced to life imprisonment, but released along with 1,149 other prisoners, including Fatah and PFLP terrorists, in exchange for three Israeli POWs. Okomoto flew off not to Japan but to North Korea, where a safe haven is provided for Japanese Red Army members. He didn't like the environment and is now cooking up mischief from a safe haven in Eastern Europe.

THE LINKAGE AMONG terrorist groups begins to seem like something out of Alice in Wonderland. I recall a relatively recent incident in which 800 pounds of explosive, stuffed into a trailer and connected to a remote-controlled, radio-activated device, was left near a leisure center on the Ormeau road in Belfast, Northern Ireland, at a time when it would have killed innumerable Christmas shoppers, Catholics and Protestants alike. The bomb-trailer was discovered, but how to keep the IRA from detonating it by remote radio control? For six frantic hours, a bomb-disposal squad, using radio frequency jamming techniques to prevent the IRA from activating the device, worked feverishly to prevent one of the biggest killer-bombs of all time from going off. When doing their dangerous work, the bomb-disposal men accept that the terrorists are probably watching their every move. Their hope was that their jamming techniques would work. They did.

The EOD team, emergency bomb disposal experts, found the 800-pound device packed with bullets and chunks of metal. The injuries would have been horrific. It was discovered that the bomb was similar to the one used in the 1984 Naples-Milan express train bombing. The explosive device was one of a number manufactured in Germany. These bombs have also been found in the possession of Mafia-connected individuals and their Neapolitan counterparts, the Camorra, in Italy. Both gangster groups sell arms and explosives to right-wing groups in

Italy as well as to left-wing groups—and to the IRA. The money for the Germany-Mafia-IRA transaction comes from the Soviet Union and Noraid supporters in America. Mindboggling?

Networking.

The KGB has the power to encourage or deter the majority of terrorist groups by opening the spigot of support or turning it off. The Western democracies can encourage or deter terrorism by their degree of support for counterterrorist activities. But the United States is in an odd position for, despite the posture assumed by the national government, individual Americans of Irish extraction remain partisans of one terrorist group, the IRA. If funds for arms stopped flowing to the terrorists from the United States, the Provos would be dependent on Libya and Moscow not just for part of their support, as now, but for all of it. What are individual Americans doing paddling in the same boat as the KGB and Qaddafi?

Let's look the facts right in the eye.

People who don't want to contribute to the IRA either in Ireland or in the United States are sometimes threatened with "punishment." The channel through which funds flow to the terrorists from the United States is Noraid, signifying North American Relief Aid.

Aid for what?

The economy of Northern Ireland is already the most aided in Europe. The United Kingdom pumps in for every man, woman and child in excess of £6,000 (approximately $9,000) per head per annum, plus enormous incentives for industry. But the function of the Noraid fundraising is not "aid" in that sense at all. It has a more sinister purpose: indiscriminate bomb attacks on bars, stores, buses, both in Northern Ireland and England. Irish terrorists do not need to hijack airplanes to make a point. They sneak into the British Isles easily enough by air or sea. Within Ireland, for them the border between North and South is a semi-permeable membrane; they are continually passing through and back. And in between the trips of the Provos, Irish men, women, and children die. Or British soldiers.

Kneecapping, aimed at potential witnesses and informants, is most effective as a terror weapon for effecting silence. Kneecapping is what it sounds like: shooting a person in the knees, which usually leaves him impaired for life. This technique scares the hell out of anyone who is even thinking of cooperating with law enforcement agencies.

The Irish have two characteristics not found in other terrorist groups. They have practically no intellectuals in their leadership, which tends to separate cause and effect and leaves the relish of action alone on the plate. Second, as Walter Laqueur notes in his book *Terrorism,* "freefloating aggression has been a frequent phenomenon in Irish history."

The Irish terrorists, in their perpetual war, have been disowned by both the Dublin and British governments. But they have not been disowned by the Americans who support Noraid.

The executive headquarters of Noraid is in Boston. The operational activity, however, finds its home in New York, where it is easier to hide. Thus the New York Police Department, particularly the intelligence unit, has put a special watch on Noraid activities that channel funds— and arms—to the Irish terrorists. (Some members of the New York Police Department, which has a large ethnic component, have lost relatives on both sides in the terrorist wars in Ireland, and are anti-Noraid.) Noraid also has major operations in Detroit and Chicago.

Noraid's supply of arms to the IRA in the last half dozen years has been made more difficult by two factors. First there has been an increase in cooperation between American and British counterterrorist authorities in attempting to stop the flow of arms and money for arms (the latter much more difficult to accomplish). Second, Noraid has had to adopt a higher profile and a more visible link with the IRA in order to achieve the level of supply necessary to maintain effective terrorist activity in Ireland.

The higher profile has come from the activities of men like Martin Galvin. Galvin is a usually well-dressed New York lawyer who is the Publicity Director of Noraid. In 1984, he traveled to Ireland to lead the annual pro-IRA rally and march at Bundoran in County Donegal. This place is just a few miles from the town of Mullaghmore in County Sligo, where Lord Mountbatten, with three others in his boating party, was murdered in 1979 by Thomas MacMahon of the IRA, using a remote-activated explosive device.

Alongside Galvin in the march was Martin McGuinness, the IRA chief of staff. And when Galvin and McGuinness stood on the platform, alongside them was Peter King, Grand Marshal of the St. Patrick's Day parade in New York City in 1984. Photographed standing together, the linkage was complete.

The event was attended by members of the New York Emerald Society police band, in defiance of a New York City ban. The parade, in commemoration of the IRA prisoners who died in a hunger strike, is a major fund-raising event for the IRA.

Americans of rank, acting out of naiveté, have been immensely helpful to Noraid. There are members of the Congress who know a lot more about backroom politics than they do about international terrorism. I use the word naive, for if they are not naive, they are abetting murderers knowingly.

Not all Americans of Irish extraction are naive on this score. A strong countervailing force has been that of Senator Daniel Patrick Moynihan, whose political astuteness extends to international affairs, with a special concern for Soviet espionage and terrorist networks. He knows what Noraid is up to and works against its nefarious purposes.

It is disconcerting to a New Zealander of largely Scots and Irish extraction like myself to find Americans of Irish origin on the other side of the fence from the FBI, which is the law enforcement agency in the United States most concerned with keeping an eye on Noraid's illegal activities. It is also surprising to find Irish-Americans on the same side of the fence as the Communist and Islamic sources of IRA arms and funds.

JUST A MONTH before the celebrated SAS attack that liberated the hostages in the Iranian Embassy in London, an SAS officer named Richard Westmacott led a raid against an IRA stronghold in a house in Belfast. Westmacott, a Guards officer attached to the SAS—his SAS affiliation was not at once publicly acknowledged—spotted the white flag being shown from the house. Responding to an ingrained sense of honor, he went forward to accept their surrender. Exposed, he was suddenly fired on by an M60 heavy machine gun that practically cut him in half. The terrorists got away with local help, but the incident stays imbedded in the minds of every counterterrorist I have ever met. *A white flag means nothing to the IRA.* The M60 heavy machine gun used to kill Westmacott was one of several stolen from a *U.S. National Guard Armory in Denver, Colorado* and smuggled to Ireland. Is the American who stole the machine guns responsible for Captain Westmacott's death? Did he transport the M60s to Ireland himself, or did it pass through a chain of willing accomplices? What that man and those accomplices need to get through their heads is that when Qaddafi cut the IRA off from the money and weapons it was receiving because the IRA *was not extreme enough,* Noraid filled the gap and became the IRA's number one source. Then when the IRA pulled off the Brighton bombing in 1983, nearly destroying the entire British government, Qaddafi smiled on the IRA again and started pumping money and arms into its terrorist activities. Thus Irish-American dollars and arms were once again mingling with money and arms from America's declared enemy and the prime mover of outrages in Europe and the Middle East. The matchmaker who got the IRA and Qaddafi back together again? Abu Nidal, the terrorist generalissimo who has replaced Carlos in the public mind as Number One on the terrorist hit parade.

I have never been face to face with Abu Nidal. I have long known him to be one of the most ruthless and effective of the Arab terrorists.

The public is finally being told some of Nidal's background, which has a similarity to that of Carlos. Carlos came from a well-to-do family, and so did Nidal. Carlos was an ideological Marxist before the acts of terrorism themselves displaced his ideology. Nidal, whose real name is Mazen Sabry al-Banna, was born in Jaffa, a Mediterranean seaport in what was then the British Mandate of Palestine, in the late 1930s. When, in 1948, the United Nations partitioned Palestine into a Jewish homeland, with the West Bank and Gaza going to the Arabs, Nidal's family found itself in what was to become Israel and, like many Palestinians, was moved out. Nidal, then still a boy, had to have felt expropriated, kicked out, his family, though wealthy, unable to preserve its place. He became, in time, the world's angriest Arab, no longer aiming for justice for the Palestinians but for preventing any move by Arabs or Israelis or Americans for peace in the Middle East. And his method is to plan the most conspicuous and costly terrorist outrages. He tasted "big blood" as part of the leadership of Black September when that group sent a hit team to Munich at the time of the Olympics, which resulted in the killing of the Israeli athletes in what is now known as the Munich massacre. By 1985, he was responsible for a majority of the front-page terrorist acts. Arafat's lieutenants have been killed on Nidal's orders. Nidal would kill Arafat himself as readily as any Israeli. The killing has displaced the original motivation. He is like the American gangsters who went on rampages in the 1930s, daring all of society to catch them, except that Nidal's

dance of death is not in a city like Chicago or over the rural
South, but in the great cities of Europe and the Middle
East.

Nidal was originally part of Yasir Arafat's PLO guerrilla operations, Al Fatah. But Nidal began to see Arafat
as "soft" (this often means "willing to negotiate") and
broke away in 1973 to set up the Fatah Revolutionary
Council. In December of that year, the United States was
preparing to sponsor a conference in Geneva to seek a
means toward peace in the Middle East. *That is not what
Nidal wants.* His men killed thirty-one people in an attack
on a Pan Am plane in Rome. The list of outrages carried
out by Nidal's faction since, culminating in the Vienna
and Rome airport attacks just after Christmas 1985, would
take pages. One is worth mentioning because it throws
light on how linkage works, how Nidal became interested
in helping Irish terrorists.

In 1982 Nidal's hit team shot Shlomo Argov, the Israeli
Ambassador to London, in the head. He has never fully
recovered. Nidal's assassins were caught and jailed in the
United Kingdom. Nidal is determined to secure their
release. In the meantime, Britain has become one of his
many priority targets. Britain's relatively minor involvement in the Middle East peace process angers Nidal
further. Counterterrorist sources in Europe learned that if
the talks in London between Palestinian representatives
and the British, based on Jordan's initiative, had continued, Nidal intended to kill the Palestinians. Nidal has
sentenced Arafat to death. Arafat has sentenced Nidal to
death. Nidal considers the peace-seekers to be traitors. One
must ask, traitors to what? Surely not the Arab cause.
Perhaps traitors to the ideal of escalating terrorism as the
controlling warfare in the world. Nidal's hatred is historic
and cast in stone.

To prove his position, Nidal has already murdered PLO
representatives in Germany, Greece, Portugal, and Lebanon. Nidal's anger was also evident when Anwar el-Sadat

got involved in the Camp David peace process. Yousef el-Sebai, an Egyptian newspaper editor and a close friend and advisor of Sadat, was targeted by Nidal in Cyprus, shot, and killed.

To terrorists one of the advantages of linkage is having a home away from home. Carlos, a Venezuelan, operated out of Paris for a considerable period of time. Nidal, until about 1980, operated out of Baghdad, the capital of Iraq. Iraq is a conservative Arab state, totally opposed to Israel. When Iraq had had enough of Nidal, it deported him. Nidal found sanctuary in the Soviet Union's most important puppet state in the Middle East, Syria. While Nidal still maintains a headquarters for his faction in the Bekaa Valley of Lebanon, which is under Syrian control, at this writing he himself is headquartered in Damascus and Tripoli. It is from there that he planned and executed his 1985 outrages.

IT HAS BEEN said of the Russian Revolution that it ate its children. The fact is that it ate not only its children but many who could have been considered its parents.

There are parallels in the international terrorist movement. Abu Nidal kills Arab children by enlisting and training them for suicide missions when they are not yet of an age to understand the full import of surrendering one's life. Nidal's "parent," against whom he has turned, is Yasir Arafat.

As Arafat veered toward diplomacy, uncompromising offshoots rebelled against any solution to the Palestinian problem that didn't include the extermination of Israel. Black September and other exotically named terrorist groups sometimes embarrass the PLO in the diplomatic arena with their violent acts of terrorism. In terms of uniting disparate terrorist movements around the world, the most important group formed after the 1967 Six Day War was the PFLP, the Popular Front for the Liberation of Palestine, led by Dr. George Habash, whose aim was to unite all of the Arab states of the Middle East as a step toward a Marxist world revolution. The PFLP's aims were the elimination of capitalism, but before that came the destruction of Israel. Habash's deputy and field commander, Dr. Wadi Hadad, was instrumental in establishing links with terrorist groups in North Korea, Japan, Europe, and Latin America. El Fatah fathered the PFLP and Black September. In the Entebbe incident, the PFLP combined Germans and Palestinians again under the leadership of the Venezuelan Carlos. Japanese were used by the PFLP for the Lod airport massacre. Hadad's internationalist arms embraced Turks and Iranians, European terrorist groups, and the IRA.

As the PLO sought to link Arab interests for the liberation of Palestine, the PFLP sought to link terrorists of all nationalities in an international consortium of terror whose ultimate aim was a Communist victory worldwide. With a core of Al Fatah personnel and preachings from the historic Moslem Brotherhood, Habash and Hadad created the most effective of the terrorist organizations—if publicity is the measure of success—through the Lod and Munich massacres via Black September, the spectacular OPEC kidnappings, and the vicious murder of U.S. Ambassador Clee Noel in Khartoum.

Perhaps the success of the breakaway groups spurred Arafat to think of a larger canvas. When President Reagan took office for the first time, he was outspoken in his condemnation of terrorists. Arafat's response was a threat of action against U.S. military bases. "We are a great revolution that can never be intimidated," he said. "We have connections with all revolutionary movements around the world, in Salvador, Nicaragua—and I reiterate Salvador—and elsewhere in the world." Arafat is a seasoned exponent of political rhetoric.

People have short memories. Today, Arafat's peacenik disguise works in circles high and low. When he addressed the United Nations in 1974, the gun he carried showed.

What would the U.N. General Assembly have made of any other "diplomat" addressing it gun on hip?

Arafat's strategy has always been to receive the public "credit" for terrorist actions taken by others. When a train-load of Jews fleeing the Soviet Union was attacked on its way to Vienna, credit was claimed by a group that called itself, for publicity purposes, the Eagles of the Palestinian Revolution. They were PLO. When five Saudi diplomats were kidnapped in Paris, the terrorists who took credit called themselves Al Iqab, a name not heard before or since. They were, of course, PLO. I have heard otherwise intelligent people say, "But Black September isn't Arafat!" though both the Sudanese and Jordanian governments have revealed documentary evidence that Black September was no more an independent group than Joseph Colombo's Italian-American cultural organization was independent of the Mafia. Even when an important Black September leader decided to reveal his connection to Arafat, there were those who preferred to believe the fiction that there was no link between the two.

People who remain politically innocent would like to think that the PLO is substituting diplomacy for terrorism. If that were the case, what could possibly be the reason for the PLO purchasing the duty-free gift shop at Tanzania's Dar es Salaam international airport? Could it be that the gift shop's customers have passed through security to get to the duty-free shop, which might just be able to supply them with a few things for their plane ride that might have set off the security alarms? Conveniently, the duty-free shops get their merchandise from trucks that do not get a going over by security. And is it true that the PLO is actively trying to buy other such shops at airports in other African countries? If it is, those of us intent on the prevention of terrorist acts have new worries.

The fact is that in anyone's estimate, the PLO's militant offshoots constitute some of the most important terrorist groups in the world, even if they occasionally shoot at each other instead of the rest of us. Americans in particular should remember that when Arafat threatened President Reagan, it was with retaliation in Salvador and Nicaragua, a world away from Palestine. This is another example of linkage between causes that have the common ground of being anti-American. It is in pursuit of his anti-American policy that Qadaffi has recently poured millions into Nicaragua.

Linkage is important also because terrorism is warfare by proxy, a process becoming more and more refined within the power plays in our modern world.

Walter Laqueur, in his book *Terrorism,* shows how the Russian terrorists of 1881 inspired the Fenians and the Anarchists, how the Russian Social Revolutionaries, the nineteenth-century Italian terrorists, and the early IRA "found imitators in many parts of the world." The leaders of the Armenian terrorist movement came to Turkey in 1892 from Russia. These terrorist groups had *their* cause. For the last quarter of a century, terrorists have been fighting the causes of others because their means has become an end. We have Palestinians killing in Paraguay and France; Japan's Red Army Faction operating in Kuwait and the Netherlands as well as in Israel; German terrorists turn up in Sweden, kill in France, and link up with Arabs under Ugandan "protection." French terrorists kill in Belgium on behalf of their Belgian friends. The coordinators and paymasters of international terrorism are the oil-rich Libyans, the North Koreans, and the Iranians, all with some form of extreme world revolution in mind, all with the tacit support of the Soviets with their highly active GRU and KGB coordinators at strategically placed embassies such as Athens. The Soviet design is of course a more calculating and rational one. All forms of disruption in the West, no matter of what origin, can to them be only conducive to the eventual defeat of Western democracy.

One can say that what unites the fanatical terrorists

who are Arabs or Persians is Islam, where death rushes the warrior into the arms of his Maker and provides him with a place in an everlasting Paradise. But we can all observe that Khomeini's religious fervor—directed against women and intellectuals as well as heretics—has nothing to do with militantly anticlerical Soviet atheism. And that those who wish to see the world turn Red—Japanese, Nicaraguan, German, Cuban, French, Basque, and American Marxist terrorists—have nothing to do with Islam. Does it confound our understanding to ask what Italian fascists and American white supremacist groups like the Order, the Brotherhood, the KKK, and Posse Comitatus, have to do with either Marxist or Islamic terrorists?

The chief supplier of funds for the December 1985 terrorist outrages at the Rome and Vienna airports, Qaddafi, also supplied five million dollars to Louis Farrakhan, the American black leader who said, on a radio broadcast on March 11, 1984, that "Hitler was a very great man," and on July 22, 1985, in Washington, D.C., said the United States government "is the number one enemy of freedom-loving peoples on the earth." Qaddafi is privy to the opinion poll that Farrakhan "was favorably perceived by 54% of the blacks who had heard of him." Farrakhan is given to not only anti-American and anti-Semitic remarks, he attacks blacks who disagree with him in words that should be weighed: He said (about the black mayor of Philadelphia), ". . . we will tar and feather them, we will hang them from the highest limbs. We will chop off their heads and roll them down the streets." That is not the language of politicians but of extremism, and we can begin to see the link that causes Qaddafi to dig into his pocket for five million dollars for the further work of Farrakhan.

Qaddafi, who has boasted about his state-sponsored terrorism, is dependent on the expertise of certain American companies for getting his oil out of the ground and, with the proceeds, funding terrorist activity. Those companies include Amerada Hess, Chevron, Conoco, Marathon, and

Occidental Petroleum. I have watched news broadcasts about American students staging protests to cause their universities to divest themselves of shares in companies trading with the Apartheid government of South Africa. I have yet to see those students—or anyone else for that matter—staging protests to cause their universities to divest themselves of shares held in companies that do business with killer Qaddafi.

IT IS A great temptation to distinguish between terrorist groups, to find some more "acceptable" or less reprehensible than others. Politicians are especially good at this when it suits their purpose. Yet the fact is that a German will kill a French general, a Spaniard will kill French holidaymakers, an Irishman will kill a potpourri of shoppers, an Armenian will kill German migrant workers, a Japanese will kill Italian businessmen—all are guilty of slaughtering victims who are removed both philosophically and geographically from the arena of the protested cause. Terrorism is indiscriminate. We should not play the game of discriminating among—and grading—terrorist groups. There are no "good" terrorists because their cause is "good." All terrorists are the enemy.

What links the individuals in all the terrorist groups around the world is their distaste for the democratic process, their intense hatred of their perceived enemies. Their common desire is to destabilize the Western democracies, especially America because of its leadership role. And finally, what links them is their obsession with violence against human beings, shooting, maiming, blowing up. The terrorist act becomes their cause and their craze, their ideology, and their religion. They can therefore link hands and arms and funds with the like-minded.

It has been said with justice that if all political action is laid out not in a straight line but in a circle, the extremists of the far right and far left will meet; they are more like each other than the rest of humanity that inhabits the other parts of the circle. The same analogy can be made for the terrorists who have networked their way around the globe in opposition to the rest of mankind, which would like to live in peace, with a reasonable expectation of dying in bed of old age instead of in an airport lounge from bullets that reached their destination through the multinational links of world terrorism.

6

The Vulnerability
of the World:
New Weapons of Terror

I have personally viewed in Amsterdam the specification sheets for six kinds of nuclear devices that are being offered for sale at a very high price.

The public is understandably concerned about nuclear devices getting into the hands of terrorists. I have to report that in the terrorists' arsenal there are weapons of less dramatic appeal that are in many respects worse. They are readily available to terrorists and most *have already been used against selected targets.* They vary from crude bombs to the latest in sophisticated timing devices and the use of deadly toxins.

The terrorist's purpose is to manipulate people's dread of random destruction. To understand the terrorist's mindset with regard to the new weaponry, one must first consider a marked change in strategy that makes it likely that the terrorists will be using the new weapons as they can.

Just as the terrorist thinks only of the terrorist, the criminal takes only his own fate into consideration. Therefore, when in 1985 William Tucker, in his book, *Vigilante:*

The Backlash Against Crime in America, pointed out that young muggers in the United States were finding it to their advantage if caught to have killed their robbery victims, the people who were potential victims of mugging would understandably be more terrified than before of being mugged. Previously, death in a mugging—if resistance were offered—might be accidental; now it was part of the mugger's plan.

In the terrorist world there has been a similar escalation. Five terrorist groups, the French *Action Directe*, the Italian Red Brigades, the Belgian CCC (Cellules Communistes Combattantes), the West German RAF (Red Army Faction), and the Greek N170 (November 17th Group), announced in 1985 a new offensive with a policy of shoot-to-kill assassinations in preference to the taking of hostages. Three of the five have already carried out assassinations. This cannot but help to increase the level of fear in potential victims, especially since the groups have announced the policy publicly and formed an alliance to execute the policy. They will now monitor each other's adherence to the new, harsh rules.

The most important strategy that the more than fifty groups that I keep track of have in common is creating fear, fear of being taken hostage, fear of of instant, unwarranted, random death. Only those who take comfort in fatalism can shrug their shoulders at the threat. And those individuals who are in specially targeted groups—diplomatic and military personnel, businessmen of high station, Americans, Israelis, and Jews worldwide—are particularly vulnerable. However, before the reader takes comfort from not belonging to one of the specially targeted groups, he will do well to remember that terrorist actions by their nature take lives at random. The majority of those killed by the Arab-sponsored Japanese-executed attack on civilians at Lod Airport in Tel Aviv were Puerto Rican Christians. We must constantly face the fact that terrorists are conducting a war against the world, and that is what makes their new weapons frightening indeed.

BEFORE I PREOCCUPY the reader with the new weapons of terror, we need some perspective on the older weapons, and particularly the machine gun or automatic rifle, the latter being a hand-carried machine gun and the most used weapon of terrorists today. That invention is exactly one hundred years old and is presumed to have already killed more people than any other weapon in the history of mankind.

Hiram Maxim, a Maine-born Yankee, was an inventor of gadgets, some of which proved important in the history of the world. For instance, Maxim was responsible for the first electric lights in a New York City building. His method of hardening the carbon filaments of light bulbs may have contributed more than the devotees of Edison might be willing to admit. In 1882, Maxim was in Vienna. There he met a fellow American who said, according to Maxim, "Hang your chemistry and electricity! If you want to make a pile of money, invent something that will enable these Europeans to cut each others' throats with greater facility."

Inside of three years Maxim developed the world's first practical machine gun. There are two important points to note about this weapon. Even at today's prices, the best .50-caliber heavy machine gun costs only about $5,000. The automatic assault rifles most frequently used by terrorists cost only the equivalent of a few hundred dollars apiece. Very few machine guns end up on the scrap heap. If damaged, they are easy to repair and recycle.

What makes the hand-carried machine gun or automatic rifle more terrifying than a rifle or pistol that fires one shot at a time, is that the automatic rifle spreads bullets at the rate of several per second, thus enabling the holder to kill or maim a large number of people standing in an airport lounge, for instance, within seconds.

We now move on to the escalator of terror to consider the rigging of a conventional weapon—the hand grenade—into an instrument of potential terror. I am speaking of booby traps.

Early in my career, when I was a specialist with the Commonwealth forces fighting in Vietnam, I had some unwelcome experience with terrifying booby traps, including some of ingenious design.

A booby trap is really a part of psychological warfare that also kills. Men on one side rig a device that a man on the other side thinks he can defuse. The man on the other side has learned to be careful of dead bodies, for they can be easily rigged with a booby trap that will explode when the body is touched or rolled over. A soldier may touch a dead body with his rifle butt to be sure it is dead. That may be enough to cause the booby trap on the body to explode. It is also a duty to examine a dead enemy's pockets for intelligence information. That can lead to self-destruction if the body has been booby-trapped. What I encountered in Vietnam were ingenious booby traps offering themselves for easy defusing. The problem was that as you defuse the visible, another explosive device nearby is set off by your very action of defusing the first device. If you encounter enough booby traps, especially those concocted by the ingenuity of a mind with long practice in deception, you begin to feel that you are engaged in a kind of Russian roulette, and that however skilled you are in defusing explosives, you will eventually encounter one that will fool you, which you will know only for the split second of the surprise detonation. In fact my most serious injury came about when not I but someone in my party accidentally stepped on a hidden explosive and some of the shrapnel found its way into me.

The terror aspect of booby traps escalated in recent years when the Soviets started to use booby-trapped toys in

Afghanistan. These were frequently dropped from planes in populated areas and looked like toys. Children, of course, picked them up and were blown to bits. The terror, of course, is designed to get at the parents, and it does.

The principle of booby-trapped bombs now has reached a level of sophistication that is much enjoyed by some terrorists. For instance, in Ireland and elsewhere, bombs have been planted in dark places with photoelectric cells that will respond to a flashlight in the hand of a member of an antibomb squad by blowing up not far from the hand holding the flashlight or the face searching the darkness. Explosives also come equipped with trembler devices that are sensitive to the slightest movement. You try to work on defusing the bomb, and your first touch is rewarded with the explosion you were trying to prevent.

In the nineteenth century, a terrorist would *throw* a homemade bomb or fire a pistol to assassinate a specific person. John Wilkes Booth used a pistol when he shot President Lincoln in his box at Ford's Theater. Today it would be possible to kill Lincoln by simply rigging his chair with a pinlike object carrying a minute capsule of ricin. This would puncture his posterior when he sat down, and the capsule would break off and remain in his body. The assassin would have long vanished. All he would need to know is which seat the President was going to occupy. Ricin, which is a poison ten times as potent as cobra venom, has already been used by a terrorist to kill an important person not in Transylvania somewhere, but in central London.

You will recall that an intelligent and knowledgable defector from Bulgaria named Georgi Markov became a broadcaster to his native land on the BBC World Service. Then, on September 8, 1978, Markov was standing on the sidewalk on Waterloo Bridge, London, when a man bumped into him and touched him with the point of his umbrella, jabbing a pellet containing a tiny amount of ricin into Markov's thigh. Had the Bulgarian operative administered a somewhat higher dose, Markov would have died almost instantly. *But they didn't want Markov to die immediately.* They wanted a chance for their assassin to get away and perhaps for Markov to experience the four days of excruciating agony he went through before he died.

On October 12, 1984, the IRA, in an attempt to blow up the heads of the British government and destabilize Europe in one stroke, planted a bomb with a sophisticated ninety-nine-day timer, calibrated in minutes, in a Brighton Hotel where the British government was planning to house the prime minister and her cabinet during the Conservative party conference.

I know personally that security for that conference was poor in relation to the potential danger. Because of the sophistication of the timing device, hotel security was breached long before the security screen was activated. Not only did the IRA have knowledge of the conference location long in advance, they also knew the weaknesses in the explosive-detecting equipment to be used in the security sweep. They successfully concealed a large amount of powerful explosive in a wall. Someone stayed in that room long enough to do an excellent plastering job. Fortunately, the IRA did make a significant mistake. The bomb was placed against an interior reinforcing wall that forced the explosion outward. Had the bomb been properly placed, the explosion would have been contained and directed vertically through the building, causing the violent rupture of the internal structure. This, with the simultaneous blast effect, would certainly have taken many more lives. The IRA was cheated of its result by the blast being deflected out through the front of the building. This meant that the structure collapsed toward the front, leaving floors and vital inner walls weakened but intact.

This well-planned and cowardly act of assassination would have had horrendous consequences worldwide, beyond the twisted comprehension of the IRA planners.

One might suspect that the act was sanctioned by more worldly political minds. International terrorism has become too coordinated for this plan to have been confined to IRA discussion. One thing can be concluded from this: but for extreme luck or even a miracle, for the first time in the history of the world the complete government of an important nation would have been destroyed in one blast. If the enormity of all this does not concentrate the minds on both sides of the Atlantic to wipe out the IRA, then nothing will.

It ought to be recognized that the IRA could have used alternative methods at its disposal. The fact that a massive and dramatic propaganda effect was the priority dictated otherwise. A hotel employee could have been used to administer a deadly toxin such as botulism to the hotel's water supply, with the prospect of silently killing everyone in the hotel.

Consider the dangers of the poison, ricin, already in the hands of terrorists. Yet neither Britain nor the United States is currently working to develop an antitoxin for ricin with any urgency. The facilities for doing this are available and ready within the United States. But the army doesn't admit the need for the antitoxin, and its attitude is to keep this item as a running part of the army's research and development program; yet the solutions have been found through civilian resources. The army has not authorized them to manufacture the antitoxin although it is urgently needed by the antiterrorist forces and by the heads of government.

There are, incidentally, only two sources of ricin production, the United States and the U.S.S.R., although the capability to produce it does exist in the United Kingdom at a specialized government establishment. The Soviets supplied the Bulgarians with the ricin that was administered to Georgi Markov in the middle of London.

Three other cases can be cited where ricin has been used effectively. In October. 1978, Mr. Vladimir Simenov, another Bulgarian defector, was found dead in his London home, only a month after the Markov attack. In Dallas, Texas, on February 12, 1986, a Bulgarian exile, Vasil Kazashky, was attacked in an underground parking lot near the north Dallas hotel where he worked. The attacker stabbed him with an unknown object. Kazashky, a physicist in his homeland, tore off his shirt and at once sucked most of the poison out of his arm, so saving his life. Only a month earlier, another Bulgarian, Vladimir Kostov, was stabbed in the back in Paris. A pellet identical to the one used on Markov was found in the wound. Kostov became very ill—but survived. So ricin has found its place in the arsenal of terrorism.

What makes ricin a most fearsome weapon of assassination is its ease of application in such minute doses. You don't have to wait around to detonate anything. You don't have to hijack an airplane or try to get past ground security to shoot it down with a ground-to-air missile.

We have seen that ricin could have been used instead of a bomb in Brighton to eliminate the head of the British government or, indeed, much of the cabinet as well. The IRA, which has absolutely no scruples about the kind of terrorist weapons it uses, could also have used another toxin, that of botulism. By getting a quantity of botulism into the Brighton water supply—easy enough to accomplish—they would have created a situation of terror in the entire town when the disease took hold, with a great many people getting deathly ill at about the same time, not from each other but from their common water supply. It takes time to determine the cause of an epidemic like that. It takes more time to be sure of its source. But cutting off the source—the water supply of a city—creates a new emergency. Water would have to be brought in from other sources, but some people would be suspicious of *any* water with a full-blown botulism epidemic in town. People must have water to live. Some would flee Brighton. The panic could be severe. A situation of terror might envelop the entire town.

Of course the conference would have to be aborted. But canceling the conference or changing its locale would demonstrate the power of the IRA, even though the prime minister and her cabinet would have escaped harm. And what would happen to the people in the substitute town chosen for the conference? Would they fear that the terrorists would now poison *their* water? Would the very choice of a new location cause a new public terror without it being necessary for the IRA to take any new action? Would the Prime Minister fear that the choice of any location would turn the people in that location against the government?

Let us glance for a moment at a different scenario. The botulism is administered not into the water supply of Brighton, but by a kitchen worker, say, into the water supply of the hotel. Or the food. Or both. That might be much more efficient than a bomb and create an even greater amount of terror. Are the Prime Minister and her Cabinet to employ tasters, as the rulers of old had to? Or will the "tasters" be chemists who will have to examine everything they propose to eat or drink? And can anyone govern with a clear mind under those conditions?

The skeptic says, "All right, the Markov case proves that terrorists can use ricin, but botulism as a terrorist weapon is a figment of Rivers's lively imagination." Not too long ago the West German police stormed into an apartment and found a laboratory setup in which two scientists working for the Red Army Faction had been experimenting with botulism toxin.

Ricin and botulism seem like exotic tools for terrorists. Actually, there are hundreds of ordinary over-the-counter medications that can be used to create a wave of terror in a large population, witness the two Tylenol recalls in the United States. Tylenol is a trade name for acetaminiphen. The drug has been in use for many years in combination with other painkillers. In 1982, seven people in Chicago died when they took Tylenol capsules that had had the medication in the capsule replaced with cyanide by a terrorist who has never been tracked down. Tylenol was withdrawn from shelves all over the United States at a cost of tens of millions of dollars. Hundreds of millions were then expended by all makers of over-the-counter medications and vitamins to seal bottles and packages against tampering. While no such packaging is tamper-*proof,* they are tamper-resistant. Yet in February 1986 a woman in Yonkers, New York, died from taking two cyanide-laced Tylenol capsules. The government caused the medication to be taken off shelves—and asked people to destroy any capsules they already owned—because tests revealed cyanide in another location than the one where the unfortunate woman had bought hers. And some of it was in as yet apparently unopened tamper-resistant packages!

Theories have been advanced that someone seeking revenge on the makers of Tylenol might be the perpetrator or it might just be a mad crank. Incidents of this sort, of course, inspire imitators. Three more over-the-counter capsule products in common use—made by a different manufacturer than Tylenol—were taken off the market when rat poison was found in capsules that had been tampered with. Think of what terrorists might do by putting cyanide or other poison in a variety of over-the-counter medications in different parts of the country at the same time. This scenario, when it involves the terrorist mind, is horrific and very plausible.

IT IS NUCLEAR weapons in the hands of terrorists that seems to worry the public most. I have heard the question dozens of times from voices strained with fear: "What if some terrorists get hold of a nuclear bomb?"

The Israelis, as you may know, have at least ten nuclear bombs. Following World War II, the Israelis used terrorism against both military and civilian targets to achieve the conversion of British-occupied Palestine into an independent Jewish state. After the experience of the Holocaust, their mind-set for self-preservation was fierce. If it looked like Arab armies were going to push Israel into the sea, can there be any doubt that the Israelis would use their bombs?

All of the material for those bombs was taken by subterfuge from the United States and France. But a lot more fissionable material has disappeared from American nuclear facilities than went to make up the Israeli bombs. Where is it? Who has it? How might it be used?

First, let's get rid of some wrong assumptions. Nuclear explosives do not need to be dropped as bombs from airplanes. The nuclear warheads designed for artillery shells can easily fit into a suitcase. They can travel from country to country in diplomatic pouches, which are not subject to customs inspection. Moreover, when the United States becomes the primary target for terrorist warfare, nuclear devices won't have to cross any borders. The material is in the country, and the terrorists who are mentally prepared to use it are already in the United States.

But before dealing with that, there is something that we counterterrorists know that should be known by the public. *You do not need a nuclear device to create a radioactive explosion.* A conventional bomb of the kind used by car bombers or by the IRA or Italian terrorists—in fact it need not be half as large—set off in a nuclear power facility already in place, would cause an explosion that would carry a high level of radiation over a wide area. If the Soviet Union started to send nuclear missiles in the direction of the United States, presumably there would be an attempt at massive evacuation of potential nonmilitary target areas. But evacuation couldn't possibly work in the case of a terrorist use of a conventional bomb to set off a nuclear power plant explosion because *there would be no advance warning.*

I am skeptical when I hear specialists discuss countermeasures to implement public safety after a major radiation leak. There is available an antiradiation-sickness pill. It is a tablet made of potassium iodate that saturates the thyroid gland with iodine, which theoretically prevents the absorption of iodine 131 present in radiation fallout. Essentially, it would have to be taken by every endangered person before exposure or within two hours of suffering exposure. It could also be taken by high-risk groups before exposure if a threat was known and a possible explosion in the vicinity imminent. But the pill provides no protection against radiation burns on unprotected bodies and tends to cause intense nausea if taken on an empty stomach. Therefore, although mass distribution of the pills would not be impractical, the ensuing panic that would be an unfortunate reality of any evacuation would be worsened by this nausea. This could have a direct effect on two major considerations, crowd and traffic control. However, as I have said, terrorists strike without warning, rendering most of these countermeasures impractical.

The public should also have a clear sense of what today's nuclear devices are like. Forget the atomic bombs in their large casings used at Hiroshima and Nagasaki. The nuclear warhead of an MX missile has the destructive power of 300 kilotons (30 times the power of the Hiroshima bomb) and yet measures only two by three feet and weighs little more than a man. Any man who can carry another man is strong enough to carry a nuclear warhead of this kind. And the cone-shaped kind that is fitted to the head of artillery shell is small enough to go into an overnight bag.

What is being done about this?

There are in the United States two Nuclear Emergency Search Teams (NEST for short) one based at Andrews Air Force Base outside Washington, D.C., and the second at McCarren International Airport in Nevada. The specialists in NEST are trained to find and disarm nuclear devices. Its key personnel include such people as Bernard J. O'Keefe, who worked on the Nagasaki bomb.

Why do I find little comfort in the existence of this organization? Because no United States organization has been successful in stopping the horrendously large drug traffic. How on earth can one reasonably expect a law enforcement organization to stop the more highly skilled traffic in nuclear materials if they can't stop the flow of drugs, much of it carried by mere amateurs? As previously pointed out in the case of the United States, the ingredients are already within its borders as are the terrorist minds capable of using them.

I MENTIONED EARLIER that while in Amsterdam I was shown, via specification sheets that were technically authentic, six different kinds of nuclear devices. The announced price for each such device is very high, but if Libya is willing to pay Abu Nidal some $13 million a year for his lower-register terrorism, price should not be a deterrent. The deterrent is that Qaddafi doesn't know if the sellers are fronts for careless idiots or Allied intelligence operatives setting out bait to measure the degree of interest among certain prospective customers.

Which terrorists are prepared to use nuclear devices?

Within the United States there is a white supremacist group called The Order, which has ties to a similar group called The Brotherhood, and both groups are now tied, according to sworn testimony, to the Klu Klux Klan, the largest and most durable antiblack, anti-Semitic, anti-government group whose membership extends throughout many northern as well as southern states. It is significant in the context of this book to note that segments of the KKK have discarded their hooded white robes in favor of camouflage combat dress.

A captured member of The Order, one Thomas Allen Martinez, after being guaranteed the services of the U.S. government's Witness Protection Program, provided testimony that led to the indictments in early 1985 of twenty-three members of the organization, which included the terrorist killers of Denver radio commentator Alan Berg and those who held up two armored cars, one in Ukiah, California, yielding nearly four million dollars and the second one yielding half a million more. These men are also suspected of having murdered one of their own members who was thought to have "turned."

Two things are significant about these indigenous American terrorists, who are white and mostly middle class, and not as easy to spot as swarthy Mexican or Arab terrorists. They are establishing links with European terrorists, particularly the IRA and certain Marxist groups.

Most of the twenty-three indicted white supremacists have been caught, and some have been sentenced to very long jail terms after trial. But my concern is with the number on the loose, who have established training camps in the United States and assembled caches of formidable arms. I have personal knowledge of the activities of some of these homegrown U.S. terrorists, and I find the most frightening aspect of their intentions is what one of them revealed during an interrogation by federal authorities that I was privy to: *He said their intent was to activate a nuclear device.*

It wouldn't have to be smuggled in by Soviet ship.

It is already in the United States, and there is an organization prepared to use it.

THE POINT I would most like to get across to the public is that machine guns, automatic rifles, booby traps, hand grenades, ricin, botulism, and nuclear devices are all weapons that terrorists can use. We would need a thousand elaborate setups to try to stop the flow of weaponry, and in the end it wouldn't work any more than it has worked against the international drug trade. What we must do is to proceed in a preventive manner against the potential users of these weapons, for if we eliminate the terrorists we can stop worrying about whether one of them is going to terrorize or kill us with an AK-47 or a nuclear device.

The war against terrorism can be compared to the war against the narcotics trade. The relentless greed and disregard for human suffering shown by narcotics chiefs with their corrupt foreign government backers has led to the strongest pressure by the American authorities to locate and destroy the sources and distribution networks of the drugs. The war against terrorism must also be taken to the terrorist. Not only are they equal to the scum of the drug trade, they are more deadly, the aims of the governments that shield them more sinister. Whatever their original cause and motivation, they eventually become addicted to their own supply. Without killing and administering fear, they cannot survive. The U.S. Mediterranean Fleet is not required to beat the terrorist enemy. That is overkill. But standing back in horror and consternation after viewing the latest bloody atrocity on TV is not enough. You, but for the grace of God, could have been part of it.

It is not enough for politicians to denounce the outrages and offer sympathy. The politicians must be told that you, their public, expect to hear of positive action against terrorists and of the use of specialist counterterrorist forces on the ground. The expertise is there in most places. Where it is lacking, it needs to be created. Those politicians misguided enough to assist terrorism—such as demonstrated by President Mitterand in France granting amnesty to known terrorists who subsequently killed again, and those American senators obstructing known IRA terrorists from being extradited to face justice—must have their motives questioned. Do they have the deaths of innocent people on their conscience, or are they so divorced from reality and too immersed in self-interest to care?

7

The Special Vulnerability
of America

Every schoolchild in Europe and the United States, perhaps in the world, knows that Christopher Columbus discovered America in 1492.

What those schoolchildren don't know is that nearly five hundred years later, a direct descendant of Columbus was killed on a street in Madrid by Basque terrorists because he was a symbol of the Spanish link to America. Terrorists often view killing as a symbolic act the way practitioners of voodoo will stick pins in a doll-sized effigy of their enemy. Columbus's descendant, whose full name was Cristóbal Colón de Caravajal, and his driver were killed by a hand grenade and machine-gun bullets as he was being driven on a residential street on the morning of February 6, 1986.

Admiral Colón, a sailor like his ancestor, was a member of the Spanish national commission, working with counterparts in the United States, preparing the way for the five hundredth anniversary of Columbus's voyage of discovery. The admiral himself was in charge of constructing replicas of the Niña, the Pinta, and the Santa Maria, which are intended to duplicate Columbus's crossing. The Admiral's son, a lieutenant also named Cristóbal Colón, had been picked to be the captain of the Santa Maria for its 1992 crossing.

I have had a long-standing involvement with the killers of Admiral Colón. The intent of the Basque terrorists is not just tribal separatism from the rest of Spain, but to institute a Soviet-style government within the present Spanish borders. That was what the Spanish Civil War was about, fascists fighting communists for control of Iberia. The real losers were the Spanish people and democracy. That bloody conflict led to decades of Franco's dictatorship and finally to a restoration of democracy. The Basques have started another Spanish Civil War not with the costly facing off of armies, but in the cost-effective way of terrorism.

THE POST-FRANCO government in Spain was relatively tolerant of the Basque separatists, whose terrorist arm is known as ETA, until one unit, with the help of an IRA instructor, mounted a Soviet-designed RPG-7 miniature bazookalike antitank weapon on the back seat of a motor car and aimed it at the bedroom window of the house in which Adolfo Suarez, the then Prime Minister, was sleeping. The rocket hit the wall just below the window. Because only one of the two safety and arming devices on the RPG-7 rocket had been operated, it did not explode. The Basques had the will to kill the head of state, but their lack of expertise in armaments failed them. That time. And it got the Spanish government into a fight-back mood. I was hired to plan an operation to eliminate the ETA leaders who were using the South of France as a safe hideaway. Unlike the handlers of the rocket, my team was well trained and succeeded in killing and repatriating enough of them to discombobulate the organization for a period of years. I gave details of this operation in my book *The Specialist*. In that volume, I also tell of the diabolic ETA-

conceived plan to hijack a trainload of explosives passing
through Madrid and detonate it in a tunnel under the city.
Then their friends in the international fraternity, specifically Libyans and IRA members, thought they would get a
much bigger bang for their buck by getting the explosives
onto a New York City subway train and detonating it in
mid-Manhattan, with the effect of the detonation greatly
increased by the known presence of a land fault. I can tell
you firsthand that high officials of New York's police intelligence unit and federal agencies had some sleepless
nights until the plan was aborted by letting the plotters
know that informers in their ranks had spilled the beans
and that plans were in place to avert the disaster and to
retaliate against the plotters in strength. The terrorist
world decided the price/propaganda/failure ratio was too
great.

AMERICAN COUNTERTERRORIST organizations are well
aware of how effective ETA has been in rocking Spain's
fledgling democratic government. But the average American thinks of Basques—if he thinks of them at all—as
troublemakers "over there."
    There are at least ten thousand Basques in America.
One hopes that the vast majority are opposed to terrorism.
One hopes that the vast majority of Armenian Americans
are opposed to the Armenian terrorist movement, seeking
revenge against the Turks for the slaughter of Armenians
seventy years ago. But I have seen Armenian literature
that is alarming. I know of American Jews who are ready
to condone terrorist acts of the Jewish Defense League.
And the IRA terror groups have thousands of U.S. supporters. Because the United States is a melting pot of the
world's nationalities, it is far more vulnerable to terrorism
than most Americans imagine. For one thing, in addition
to its heterogeneous population, the United States has
thousands of miles of undefended—and largely unsuper-
intended—borders, north and south.

WHEN THE STATUE of Liberty, rebuilt and refurbished, finally faces the world without scaffolding, it will still have a tear in its eye. As it stands atop Liberty Island in New York Harbor to welcome the poor and the homeless from abroad, the poor and homeless will be drifting in behind its back across the Mexican and Canadian borders, clamoring for the American dream and suffering the indignities of seizure and arrest. Meanwhile, the terrorists slip in on well-oiled tracks, all expenses paid, to corrupt and carry out atrocities. I hope no American still thinks that security guards at international airports and customs officers at border crossings will prevent as many terrorists as want to from coming in. The open society of America is a playground for the seasoned terrorist.

As I pointed out in the preceding chapter, some terrorists are already in place in the United States. The public is aware that members of the Brotherhood, as they call themselves, have been caught, convicted and jailed for murdering a broadcaster and other acts of terror. This group must not be written off as spent extremists. I warn that their career has just begun. And is the public aware that Libyan, Iranian, FALN, Cuban, and Soviet terrorists are in place in the United States, some of them unsupervised by the FBI?

Americans tend to be complacent about danger to their national security from paramilitary forces. They still expect wars to be declared the way President Roosevelt did the day after the Japanese destroyed the fleet and ground installations at Pearl Harbor. Americans still expect that if an enemy force crosses a line, as the North Koreans did when they stormed across the 38th parallel, the President will be able to rally the Allies and stem the tide.

The fact is that the terrorist war against America has been declared time and again by national leaders like Qaddafi, and Americans—not all, but the majority—have shrugged the declarations off as if they were issued by an impotent madman or had no real bearing on their lives.

And when American leaders decide to react to terrorist outrages even with slaps on the wrist (an economic sanction against terrorist havens is a slap on the wrist), its closest Allies have turned their backs on requests for cooperation. Because they know it is a futile action, a case of too little, too late.

The United States is more isolated than it thinks. It is not prepared for its status as the number one target for international terrorism.

The paradoxical position of standing in the shoes of free world leadership and simultaneously being rendered impotent by a small dedicated band of terrorists is untenable. The United States is constantly sending the signal to the Soviets that it cannot be pushed around. Its rhetoric is insulated by diplomatic standoff and an inherent desire in all concerned for peace. The vital signal is not being sent to the terrorists, for with them and their sponsors there is no insulation, no desire for peace. They want war.

Perhaps worst of all, Americans still feel that terrorism is something that happens "over there," despite the fact that Americans travel more than the people of any other nation and many of them are frequently "over there."

Let's take a look at what the death's-head statisticians have to tell us:

In the 1980s so far, well over 300 Americans have been killed by terrorist action without a drop of terrorist blood claimed by American retaliation. The particulars, of course, fade from memory quickly.

In Paris, in 1982, two American women were dining in a restaurant when terrorists cut their holiday short with machine gun fire. Nothing was done.

In Athens, 1983, an American naval officer was killed by two terrorist gunmen. Nothing was done.

In Beirut in 1983, 17 Americans were killed when a truck bomb wrecked the United States Embassy. Then a suicide truck bomber rammed the United States Marine headquarters, killing 241. In that case, two kinds of things were done. The American Navy lobbed expensive shells into the hills, to little effect. And covert retaliation took place, involving my leading a group of four Americans to a headquarters from which three Syrian field grade officers, guarded by Druze militia, were planning further outrages. We killed all three and twelve of their entourage, gathered vital intelligence, and successfully exfiltrated.

As mentioned earlier, in Rome in 1984, the Red Brigades shot and killed the American Director General of the Sinai Peacekeeping Forces, Leamon Hunt. Nothing was done.

In December 1984, in Germany, Red Army Faction terrorists, dressed in United States Marine Corps uniforms and carrying United States Marine Corps I.D. cards, parked a car loaded with explosives ten yards from the main building of the NATO training school in Oberammergau. Fortunately, the fifty-five-pound bomb failed to detonate, or America would have added to its casualties. During that same month, the Red Army Faction carried out six further bomb attacks against U.S. installations, including U.S. army motor pools, a church used by the U.S. military, the U.S. Lindsay air station at Wiesbaden, a United States Air Force communications facility also at Wiesbaden, and a United States Army intelligence office located in Dusseldorf. The bald eagle stayed high on its perch, doing nothing.

The following month, January 1985, the Red Army Faction carried out an attack on the home of the United States Consul in Frankfurt, the headquarters of the United States Army in Europe at Heidelburg, and firebomb attacks on several U.S. (and allied) targets, where security precautions were lax because the Americans still didn't fully comprehend that a war was on.

That same month the United States got lucky. A Red Army Faction team, consisting of one man and one woman and a baby carriage carrying a bomb, got close to the IBM computer center in Stuttgart. The bomb went off prematurely, killing the male terrorist. Luck is something the United States can't take credit for. As the IRA said after the Brighton bombing, "You have to be lucky always."

The next month, February 1985, Bobby's Bar in Greece, a popular hangout for U.S. servicemen, was the object of a terrorist bomb attack. Score: United States seventy-eight wounded—terrorists zero.

One month later, March 1985, a thirteen-pound bomb, cleverly disguised as a fire extinguisher, was found at an American officers' club in Stuttgart. It failed to detonate. What would the Americans do without luck?

In April 1985, a FRAP terrorist group launched a bomb attack on NATO's North Atlantic Assembly office in Brussels.

As I was reading proofs of this book, a bomb exploded in a West Berlin disco frequented by Americans. This one on April 5, 1986, killed an American soldier from Detroit and a Turkish woman and wounded more than 200 others.

As Kurt Vonnegut would say, "And so it goes."

I have conveyed a report of just a few of the attacks that occurred during a period when I was convalescing from what we politely call "accidents" in counterterrorist work. I waited for effective U.S. responses in vain, knowing the ability to respond was not there. What I have found through my involvement with American law enforcement and military agencies, who are microcosms of the public at large, is that they appear to be thoroughly behind counterterrorist activity. They want something done about the outrages. They don't want to remain sitting ducks.

WHEN AMERICA DOES react, as President Reagan did in October 1985 when he ordered the intercept of the Egyptair 737 carrying the four *Achille Lauro* hijackers and their leaders, Mohammed Abbas and Ozzudin Badrak Kan, to safety, it bravely ran the risk of the big play. The Italians had a mixed reaction. They took possession of the four hijackers. *They let their leaders go.* Washington might have foreseen that the Italians might not have the courage to go along with the big play.

That's a far cry from the Italian reaction when Red Brigades terrorists kidnapped U.S. Brigadier General James L. Dozier in December 1981. He was taken from his Verona apartment and hidden in the Italian countryside. The Italians, with American encouragement, involved more than 5,000 persons in the nationwide manhunt for Dozier and his captors. It took forty-two days, including very tough interrogation of captured Red Brigades terrorists, to zero in on the location where General Dozier was being held. Not only was Dozier found before he was harmed by the five armed terrorists guarding him, but in the tracking process more than twenty terrorists belonging to the Red Brigades or the Front Line group were captured, including Red Brigades leader Giovanni Senzani.

This shows two things. Counterterrorist action *can* be effective. Second, think how the situation has deteriorated in the less than four years between the successful operation to release Dozier and the Italian government's intentionally releasing the mastermind of the *Achille Lauro* hijacking.

The intimidation of the Italian government by Libya and terrorist factions is all but complete. Italy has a good record in dealing with its own terrorists, who have committed acts of violence there for years. But Italy is now torn apart by the largest organized crime trial in its history. That, plus the political assassinations connected with it, struck fear into the highest echelons of the government and weakened the resolve of its leaders. In the face of U.S. persistence, the Italians concerned themselves more with misplaced resistance to being "humiliated." This time the prize, the *Achille Lauro* hijackers, and the extreme action initiated by the United States in intercepting the airliner was a great enough justification for Italy to go the whole way. The prize was great enough for the Americans to set aside protocol. Having put troops on the ground in Sicily, they should have collected what they went for.

Message received: The terrorist leaders are still allowed to get away.

Americans and American leaders who are in Europe as part of NATO are, in effect, guarding their allies. Yet those American allies have allowed terrorist leaders to get away scot-free. Even such highly placed Americans as Alexander Haig, when he was Commander of the Allied Forces in Europe, was in 1979 targeted and nearly killed. Later he told a Congressional committee that thousands of terrorists were in training in Libya and the Soviet Union and its satellite states and warned that if the United States did nothing to contain the spread of terrorism, "We will find it within our borders tomorrow." He might as well have been spitting into the wind.

In the decade immediately preceding the attack on Haig, 1968-1978, the record shows that 1,275 Americans and Canadians were victims of terrorist attacks, eighty-four of them inside North America.

American tourists have shown signs of being increasingly nervous about travel abroad. In the chapter on skyjacking I have conveyed some precautionary advice. But what about the literally hundreds of thousands of U.S. servicemen and women who must travel abroad on military duty? Military personnel are choice targets for terrorists. Marines are very easy to pick out of a crowd even in civilian clothes because of their close-cropped hair.

After navy diver Stethem was brutally beaten and killed aboard TWA 847 and four marine embassy guards were gunned down off duty in a café in El Salvador, the Marine Corps, which once wore its uniforms with great pride in public, opted for security instead. Corps headquarters in Washington issued instructions in September 1985 to its personnel in guard detachments around the world to be as inconspicuous as possible when traveling and off duty. They were advised to obtain civilian passports in case passports were collected during a hijacking. They were told to keep their military identification cards, service club cards, checkbooks showing rank or military addresses, and photos in uniform in checked baggage, not on their persons. Those with identifying tattoos were urged to cover them with bandages and to wear long sleeves, though these offer only "initial concealment." When traveling in civilian clothes, Marines were advised to avoid cowboy hats or belt buckles that are worn only by Americans. Flight watches became taboo. Military rings were not to be worn. And highly shined shoes, previously a mark of pride, were to be avoided. Lastly, close-cropped hair was to be allowed to grow out as a "prudent" step. The American marine who guards embassies and other diplomatic installations abroad was suddenly forced to blend into the rest of humanity as a safety measure.

The navy and the air force followed suit and gave similar advice to their personnel. The army sent a communique to each of its nearly 800,000 soldiers, advising them on appearance and habits when traveling overseas.

But what about back home? Americans tend to forget the number of terrorist attacks that have already happened within their borders. I have talked to people who are unaware that about one hundred law enforcement officers were killed in the seventies in the United States in terrorist and politically motivated crimes. Short memories have erased the headline-making bomb attacks on power supplies, state and national capitols, university facilities doing research for the military, nuclear plants, and even the Pentagon, all inside the United States. The heroism of bomb disposal technicians continues to go largely unrecognized.

I maintain a long record of terrorist attacks on Americans that failed. Most of these have gone unreported in the United States either for security reasons or because they had coverage only in local papers. I collect the details on failed attacks because those of us who are professional counterterrorists need to know as much as possible about each operating group of terrorists as we can, and sometimes we learn more from their mistakes than their successes. And I am afraid that the terrorists are successful more often than they fail because they pick their time and targets and, as yet, we don't.

TO THE EXPERIENCED eye, it was especially appalling to watch the attempted assassination of President Reagan by John W. Hinckley, Jr., over and over again on tape both in real time and slow motion. The Secret Service did a lot that was wrong and very little that was right.

Hinckley was a deranged kid, not a Carlos, but, once inside the protective ring, a reckless amateur and a dedicated professional have similar advantages.

First of all, the Secret Service allowed the protective ring that should surround a head of state when he moves in public to be penetrated by an assortment of people who served to conceal Hinckley in their midst until it was too late.

Second, the Secret Service agents all seemed to want to protect the President, leaving everybody else vulnerable. One-third of the protecting contingent went with the President to the hospital, leaving an aide wounded and helpless on the ground; *that aide happened to be in possession of the nuclear codes for the defense of the United States.*

I noticed the way most of the remaining Secret Service agents jumped on Hinckley. What if there were a second attacker? What if this were a coordinated terrorist attack designed to kill the President and get the nuclear codes? How many readers remember the bewildered expression of the Secret Service man with the Uzi submachine gun with the public crushing in toward him? What was he supposed to do, spray the public with fire? Hinckley could easily have been a diversion. Who was on the lookout for the primary assassin? The whole affair seemed out of control.

If the American leadership is to be less vulnerable, the Secret Service had better take lessons quickly in some of the basics. The same principle applies to the protection of a President as it does to the so-called Strategic Defense Initiative: protection comes in layers so that if the outer ring is broken, a second ring will be there. And if it is the *presidential* party that is to be protected—as it *must,* given the responsibilities of some of the people in his entourage—the Secret Service needs to improve its off-camera performance if it is not again to provide us with a public spectacle of rampant disorganization in the face of one amateur gunman. The woods are full of expert gunmen. I know the Secret Service is charged with protecting too many people with too few men. That remains to be rectified but still is no excuse for almost losing the President.

A smooth, well-rehearsed security detail is a joy to watch. King Hussein, arriving at the Dorchester Hotel in London, is a classic example. Hussein, because he is a man of vision and genuinely strives to attain peace in the Middle East—a position diametrically opposed to that of the Soviet Union and the militant Arab terrorist groups—is a prime target. He is protected by several SAS-trained bodyguards. If you watch him get out of his limousine, it is not in some underground garage but in front of the hotel. He gets out with complete dignity, acknowledges the manager of the hotel who is there to greet him, proceeds through the lobby to a waiting empty lift that gets him into his suite in two and a half carefully clocked minutes without anybody in the lobby knowing what's really going on. An invisible channel has been created in the lobby. An extra man, known as "the floater," also SAS-trained, a highly proficient marksman, watches the channel through which Hussein will pass, and also his own potential targets: the man looking for his credit card, the man fiddling with his suitcase. They, and others, remain in the marksman's line of fire until Hussein has passed safely through. There is no

disruption and it all takes place in what appears to the
casual observer as an unhurried entrance of a head of state
into an hotel.

I CAN'T CLOSE this chapter without addressing the special
problems of America's greatest and most vulnerable city,
New York.

Manhattan is a narrow island, cut off from the rest of the
United States by several bridges and four tunnels. One
thriller writer had a field day demonstrating what would
happen if a well-organized dissident group with military
training cut off access to and egress from Manhattan by
seizing the bridges and tunnels and setting up headquarters at the top of the Empire State building.

Manhattan is also vulnerable because it is laced with
railroad and subway tunnels in which it is demonstrably
easy to plant explosives. Above the tunnels are the tall
buildings, swaying in the wind. The skyscrapers are especially vulnerable to fires started on the high floors, which
cannot be reached by street-level firefighting equipment.
And Manhattan has a headquarters for known subversives, including highly-trained killer operatives, from
nearly all of the nations that sponsor terrorism. Those
whose cover is employment in the United Nations Secreta-
riat are free to travel all over the United States without the
limitations that apply to embassy and consular officials.
Surveillance of such a large group is beyond the means of
the FBI or any other counterintelligence group. Besides,
why stray far when Manhattan itself is so full of tempting
targets for destabilizing the United States in full view of
the representatives of all of its allies?

At this writing, the terrorist acts that have been carried
out in Manhattan have been small beer. Some years ago a
Puerto Rican terrorist group, the FALN, blew up a number
of people at an historic site in lower Manhattan, Fraunces
Tavern where George Washington made his headquarters
for a few days and then bade farewell to his officers on

December 4, 1783. Long before Central Park was the dominion of muggers at night, several assassinations were conducted there by the predecessors of the KGB. This is all dwarfed by the dangers of today.

Fortunately, the Intelligence Division of the New York Police Department is one of the most streetwise and vigilant in the world, and profoundly concerned about the danger from terrorists. But their field is advance information. On rare occasions, policemen have managed to arrest terrorists and to confiscate bombs and guns. Ordinary policemen, however, even members of SWAT teams, are not equipped by training to deal with major terrorist outrages *before they are activated.* And New York City's safety lies in being able to prevent terrorist action by getting to the source on time and stopping it before it starts. That requires rapid response teams trained in SAS and Delta methods located both within the city, their equipment always within reach, and outside the city ready to go in at short notice. In what is allegedly peacetime, this presents jurisdictional problems. New York cops will quarrel over a robbery that takes place in a street that divides two precincts. Each of the five boroughs has its own District Attorney. Across the Hudson river lies New Jersey, a different state. Law enforcement in the United States is considered a matter to be dealt with locally. And policemen are severely restricted by law from taking any kind of preventive action.

THUS THE PROBLEM of antiterrorist security in New York City is a perfect microcosm of the problems facing the United States overall. The bringing in from outside at speed of rapid response teams has to be a federal matter. Interestingly enough, it is the Federal Marshal system that has been instrumental in penetrating the legal barriers that have obstructed the apprehension of American terrorists in recent years. The United States Marshal Service has the legally authorized role and recruiting capability for harnessing selective ex-military expertise for the counterterrorism role. The historical origins of this too-little-known service give it the *esprit de corps* necessary in such a unit to reach the high degree of dedicated training required to match and beat today's terrorists. Both Delta and the marshals need accelerated and specific training if they are to become the alert rapid response guardians of America's most vulnerable city.

Viewing the Manhattan skyline is to see one of the wonders of the world. To a trained counterterrorist, it is a frightening image of too many high-gain, cost-effective targets for terrorists to aim at.

8

The Media vs the Terrorists

The title of this chapter is no accident. Amongst the total array of the world's press, radio, and television, an infinitesimal percentage would consider itself on the side of terrorism: perhaps a few newspapers in the Arab world, the media in Iran, some dissident or extremist crank media on this side of the Iron Curtain, and some but not all of the time, the controlled press on the other side of the Iron Curtain!

The vast majority of journalists, I imagine, are as opposed to the conduct of terrorists as the rest of the people in their countries. Yet when speaking of media, the phrase "vast majority" makes little sense since the range of journalistic practice is so great. There are large circulation papers on both sides of the Atlantic (and both sides of the Pacific as well, for those who know of the huge circulation of some scandal sheets in Asia) that thrive on six-fingered hands, gruesome murders, and aberrant sex, and for whom great accidents, upheavals of nature, and upheavals of human nature in the form of terrorist outrages are all fodder for exploitation. They are balanced, not in circulation but in influence, by newspapers that pride themselves on responsibility and strive for objectivity. Between these two extremes hovers the rest of the world's press.

I have watched television in nearly a dozen countries. Where more than one channel is available, I have tried to watch the news as it is depicted by each. It amazes a nonjournalist how the same events seem so different on different channels in the same country, and for me it is most striking when it concerns a terrorist incident about which I have special knowledge. The difference between channels in the same country is even more marked when the commentators come on, when the terrorist acts are interpreted, and later, when the news shifts to reactions by political leaders in various countries. I have been in the United Kingdom immediately after a terrorist outrage and have been struck by the different points of view that can be expressed concerning a single event. I have also been in the United States after a particularly serious hijacking involving Americans and have switched back and forth in the early evening among four of the many channels—the three main networks and Public Service television—and have observed the diversity not only of opinion but of what is conveyed by the manner of coverage. Perhaps the most striking thing of all is the *extent* of the coverage day after day. If it causes me pain it is not because of the diversity, which is welcome to anyone who rejects any form of censored news in an open society. It is because I know that the success of any terrorist outrage depends so much on the kind and amount of publicity it receives.

On September 6, 1970, Black September staged a hijacking of no less than five airliners, three of which it caused to be flown to a disused airfield called Dawson's Field in Jordan. This desert location is not exactly a populous part of the world, but the TV cameras got there, and it was their presence that caused the publicity-seeking terrorists to blow up all three aircraft and put at risk the lives of 425 passengers and crew members. If the media will convey the message, the message will be staged.

Of course, the newsman's job is to ferret out the news and report it. When the news, so to speak, explodes into view, as when terrorists roll hand grenades into a crowd in front of airport check-in counters and then spray everyone indiscriminately with rapid fire from Kalashnikovs or Uzis, the newsman seeks to uncover whatever special angles he can get that another may or may not get: the tear-streaked face of a women wailing next to the body of what seconds ago was her lifelong husband; tagged, sprawled bodies seen from above; police and emergency workers rushing the wounded to ambulances; blood on the floor being mopped up the morning after. The TV newsman says he cannot *not* report. And under that shield he may not have to think about the consequences. Or he may fall back on the amoralist's ultimate saw: If I don't report it, someone else will. Or: It's my job, the boss has given me instructions—I am only following orders.

There are exceptions of course, when journalists or media chiefs find themselves victims. I have great sympathy for the American Associated Press Rome bureau chief who saw his eleven-year-old daughter, Natasha Simpson, murdered and his nine-year-old son wounded by terrorists on December 27, 1985. He will, I suspect, think about the effects of what he must report when a future terrorist attack occurs. His friends and journalistic colleagues may also be affected for a time. I have my doubts, but they may even study the recent history of terrorism and note that the main reason for the shift from rural guerrilla actions to urban terror a quarter of a century ago was not that cities have more potential corpses but greater numbers of journalists and TV cameras to mark the results and broadcast them to the world. One Latin American terrorist said that the value of even a small bomb that maims only a few in a city is worth more than dozens of bodies in the countryside. The end aim of terrorist outrages is the dissemination of the act. The longer the story runs the better, hence the taking of hostages.

In late 1985 there was a shift in the "suicide war" against the Israelis in the Lebanon. Several "suicide" attackers were caught and interrogated at length. Israeli intelligence came to the conclusion that some of the car bombers were unwilling to die and had been duped. More important, the Israelis concluded that only a minority of the suicide attackers were Shi'ite Muslims and that the majority were under the control of Syria.

However, the outside world knew very little about specific incidents in the suicide war and the nature of its transformation because the Israelis took tough steps to limit the news coming out of Southern Lebanon. Reporters were kept away from the areas where suicide attacks had taken place. The Government released no information about them. The result was a sharp falloff in these attacks. According to a senior Israeli official, "If someone mounts a suicide operation and there is no story about it in the West, then it is as though it never happened, no matter how much damage it does." Listen to his next words: "You don't do terrorism to kill people. You do it to create an echo that makes you larger than life. No echo. no success."

If the purpose of the terrorist act is coverage, what is the journalist to do whose job is coverage?

THE ISSUE HAS been raised in even more dramatic circumstances in Japan and the United States when, within the last few years in both countries, television journalists witnessed a savage crime in progress and kept the cameras rolling at a time when they might have interfered with the crime directly or by calling the police. Are we to expect more of journalists than of the thirty-eight members of the general public who saw and heard the long-drawn-out murder of Kitty Genovese on the streets of Queens in New York City and did nothing about it?

Are there circumstances where a journalist is a responsible citizen first and a recorder afterward? If he is witnessing the murder of Kitty Genovese, does he call for a photographer or the police or both? And if both, in what order?

One accepts the fact that it is the journalist's duty to report the news. But it is not the journalist's duty to make the news. A hijacked plane is news. But when hostages are taken, whether aboard a plane or anywhere else, and a siege begins, the terrorists are trying to get the media to achieve the terrorists' end: publicity. In my experience, newsmen are particularly allergic to attempts to use them for publicizing commercial products or events. It is my suggestion that they view terrorists' attempts to exploit the media for publicity purposes with the same caution and disdain.

Terrorism benefits from coverage. The best counterterrorist activity is not filmable and frequently not reportable. Therefore, in terms of the worldwide terrorist effort, coverage by news media tends to be one-sided.

There are ways in which media coverage can be helpful. When an outrage takes place, the informed reporter should give the political parentage of the terrorist group. The PLO's splinter groups, and splinters of splinters, have been amply reported, but the public needs to know more about the link-ups among the terrorists and the hierarchies. An informed public will then understand if an informed leadership takes action not just against the specific terrorists who committed an act if they are within reach, but against the men who train and plan and send young terrorists out to draw blood.

The media could contribute to the war against terrorism in other significant ways. I would like to see documentaries on the downside of terrorism, the "suicide" volunteers who didn't volunteer, images of those who have been in prison for many years, even the major informers who were once in the terrorist ranks but saw the error of their useless cause and turned against it. Above all, the terrorist must be portrayed for what he is, not a hero but a fanatic who has made violence an end in itself.

The media can also help by keeping us informed of records as they do in sports. The first killing in a particular territory is an outrage, but when, as in Northern Ireland, over a period the number of policemen, soldiers, and civilians murdered runs into hundreds, each new victim becomes merely a statistic. The resulting indifference thus ironically helps the terrorist instead of exposing him to justifiable public rage. If the reporting of an outrage gives us some of the history of other such events in that region, the continuity will be visible, and indifference will be impossible. The media, instead of exploiting a particular terrorist-staged event by giving it publicity for days on end, can be of enormous help in the counterterrorist effort by making the terrorist war visible to a public that isn't aware of it as a war.

NEEDLESS TO SAY, the kind of covert operation I specialize in is never covered by the press and cannot be. When we are successful we don't call a press conference to celebrate. We are debriefed and returned to our respective places in the world. If any of us on a mission are killed, there is no mention of it in the news. Had we been captured, our association with any government or agency would have been denied. We would have been interrogated, tortured, and killed. We would not have been taken prisoner for, unlike hostages, we are deniable people. Spies are deniable people also, but are usually exchanged eventually for spies from the other side. Counterterrorists who go on clandestine operations have no such luck. That is one reason counterterrorists need such a high degree of training. We *must* succeed because our lives are on the line even more than the lives of spies. We are not exchangeable.

We in professional counterterrorist circles are understandably apprehensive about the media. For us to continue to be effective in the field, our faces cannot be seen, little must be known about us. Even some of our closest friends do not know exactly what we do and can reach us only through cutoffs and intermediaries. Some of the organizations and countries I have worked for, to whom I am a deniable person, have been rather severe about my previous writings even under a pseudonym. The terrorist side in this war speaks to the world through the media, while the counterterrorist side is heard only through statesmen and academics whose information is worthy but usually second hand. I am attempting, at risk, to redress that balance, but I am baffled by the fact that one of the three main American networks will publicize terrorist-staged events to an extreme degree, but if a deniable counterterrorist is willing to risk exposure in order to report the other side of these outrages, the network wants a government agency to verify the counterterrorist's identity in writing! They'd have as much luck getting the CIA to give them authentication of an American covert agent in the field! Their naiveté is unbelievable.

I remain wary when it comes to the differences among the media. When I appear on television, my face is not seen, but whatever I say is heard by the public uncensored. When I speak on radio, the public actually gets to hear what I have to say. My discomfort is mainly with print because of its very nature. I am asked questions. I try to answer them as candidly as I can without betraying colleagues or friendly countries. But, not unexpectedly, what I say is distorted when it appears in print. Therefore the printed medium I prefer is a book because what I have to say appears in a form I approve of, without the hazard of distortion before my words reach the public.

In some respects I would have preferred to keep silent. A soldier is taught that, when captured, he is to give only his name, rank, and serial number. If I were to be captured on a counterterrorist mission, I would not even bother to give my name. After fifteen years of practicing silence, it has taken some persuasion by trusted colleagues for me to get involved in this discussion even anonymously. But the arguments are strongly in favor. An aware public is essential to the defeat of terrorism. I feel that politicians must take into account an aware public when making their crisis decisions. A public informed by fact, not by sensationalized journalism and endless theorizing, makes the politicians accountable.

To the journalists and cameramen reading this I say, when covering outrages remember: *The terrorists' real objective when killing and maiming is to get you to report it.* The terrorists' objective in taking hostages is to get you to report it in order that the world be terrorized by an act in one specific place. The terrorists love it when you run down the hostages' families and record their fear. To the extent that you maximize that coverage, you are playing into the terrorists' hands. Remember, terrorism exists where there is a free press *because* there is a free press. In societies where the press is censored, terrorist acts are minimal because the whole point is for news of the outrage to get about. The Soviet Union has a great advantage over the Western allies. It can fund terrorist activity with impunity, and its own territory is safe from outrages because it won't get covered in the censored press.

I am never pleased about any terrorist act anywhere, but if anything positive comes from these acts, perhaps we should look to Lebanon when, in 1985, four Soviet nationals were kidnapped in Beirut. One was killed, and the other three held hostage by Moslem fanatics. The Soviet press does not normally report bad news, but it did report this killing of a Soviet national by terrorists. The Soviets stepped up their pressure on Syria to get the remaining three released. But more important, it caused the Soviet authorities to go public in a condemnation of terrorism! By itself that one incident won't stop the Soviet support of terrorist activity in the rest of the world, but it must have given the leadership at least a moment's pause to know that they have been included in the rest of vulnerable mankind.

9

Mind-Set

Between the wild country of the Brecon Beacons in Wales (where the SAS conducts what is probably the toughest training course in the world) and the outskirts of London, there are hundreds of pubs. Many of them have a dart board, around which the locals will gather. If you listen to them, you will observe the mind-set of humanity cut in three. There are those who will say, "Watch me miss," because it is in their nature to downgrade the possibility of success; whatever good throws they manage are an improvement over their announced goal of "missing." At the other extreme are the braggarts who will say, "Treble twenty coming up," and will then blame missing their goal on some distraction or other excuse. Between these two extremes of pre-action publicity is the attitude of the man who has through willpower and training become a damn good dart thrower. He will usually say nothing as his turn comes. He will aim for the treble twenty, score well, and sit down, still inwardly critical of his performance. All three of these types are, of course, amateurs, but the attitude or mind-set of the third is the kind I identify with the profes-

sionalism of the best-trained soldier. He assumes his target
is the treble twenty, and his mission is to hit it.

There is a tendency to confuse *will* with *mind-set*. The
best will in the world can get you started, but it takes
training and experience—which means lots of expert
knowledge—to develop a mind-set that will enable you to
function effectively, whether in front of a dart board or in
front of a crisis management team responding to the latest
terrorist outrage.

A surgeon would have no trouble cutting open someone's
windpipe in an emergency if it was necessary to save the
person's life. His mind-set would enable him to do the same
if he was not in an operating room and the only tool at
hand was a pocket knife. His priority remains the saving
of life.

The same surgeon could not be expected to wield the
same knife to take a life in order to save others. His famil-
iarity with bloody detail does not automatically equip him
with the mind-set required by my profession on occasions.
The same equation relates to the politician totally familiar
with the terrorists, their mentality, and their danger to him
and society. Does he automatically acquire the mind-set
and the necessary sleight of hand to eliminate them? No, I
am afraid it does not quite work like that.

When the might of a country's air force is released, the
politician makes his decision influenced by the will of the
people and the fact that both he and the people are
informed and accept the professional skills of the pilots.
The political decision having been made, the job is then
done with every confidence in the pilot's dedication, training, and mind-set. Certain criteria have been met. The
people have recognized the threat to them and the need to
strike back. The politician receives that clear signal from
the people and brings into action the highly trained air
force with clear orders to take the fight to the enemy. The
planes are launched and everybody expects victory. It is all
tangible, the ingredients are identifiable and also a touch

glamorous. The fight is somewhat conveniently at arm's length. The visual act of launching those planes has both politician and people thinking that retaliation has been satisfied.

Counterterrorism does not provide the same kind of release because, at its best, it is a covert action and unspectacular except as to its results. But taking the war to the enemy sometimes means that the results will not be photographed by TV or reported by journalist-observers. If there is to be any acknowledgment of the event it should simply be in the form of a statement by a spokesman for the White House or some other government that such-and-such terrorist training camp or camps have been eliminated. He would answer, "No comment," to all questions, including how it was done and by whom.

The mind-set that is required to defeat terrorism today has to include the knowledge that the terrorist goes after publicity, and the counterterrorist must most often go after results that cannot be published in a way that is as useful to politicians as staging something spectacular that can be filmed and reported on.

PRESIDENT REAGAN MUST be credited for having had the will to defeat terrorism for years. It was a long time ago that he promised "swift and effective retribution" for any terrorist outrage. When TWA 847 was hijacked in June 1985, President Reagan said, "We have our limits—and our limits have been reached. This cannot continue." At one point he added, "America will never make concessions to terrorists." Yet the limits have been passed many times since, concessions have been made to the terrorists, and swift and effective retribution is, at this writing, yet to come. Clearly the President's instinct is not to be repeatedly humiliated by terrorist actions. However, he must deal not only with his own mind-set but those of his closest advisors, the not-so-close bureaucrats who have got their feet mired in diplomacy in the middle of a war, and of the people he governs. His is the position of many leaders. Actually, the people are far ahead of the politicians. The majority want something concrete done about terrorism.

Polls have shown that people react most strongly against terrorism immediately after the event. But soon the will deteriorates. Often the long delay between the atrocity and the terrorists' arrest and public trial means that the success is lost on the public.

One wants to punish the guilty, but there seems to be a conflicting demand to save the innocent. That is a false contradiction, for in fact it is only by punishing the guilty immediately that the innocent will be saved. The problem is that the "punishment" is misconceived. What is most needed is a mind-set focused on disabling the terrorists, for the moment they are disabled innocents are no longer in danger.

Long after outrages are committed, there are discussions in quarters high and low about "clean" targets, ones that won't involve innocent bystanders. In any hostage crisis the targets are clear: they are the terrorists who are holding the hostages, and the response is not to wait out the media event of the siege and then bomb a terrorist stronghold (which inevitably involves killing innocents as well) but to send in the specialists who have been trained and are ready—the rapid response teams.

The mind-set of Americans was revealed in a *New York Times*/CBS News Poll conducted in the second half of January 1986 in a manner the experts say gives you a sampling error of plus or minus three percent. That poll showed that the majority of American men—and an even larger majority of American women—believed that the United States should do more against terrorism. But the majority was also opposed to taking military action against terrorists or governments helping them because the question was put in the framework of innocent people possibly being killed. The whole thrust of counterterrorist professionalism is to kill only the guilty and prevent the same or other terrorists from claiming future victims.

On American public television, Ariel Merari, an outspoken expert on terrorism who is a professor at the Center for Strategic Studies at Tel Aviv University, said with a touch of sarcasm, "We do not allow ourselves to kill terrorists as if they are enemy soldiers." The "we" was polite, for it is the Americans, not the Israelis, who still have trouble thinking of terrorists as soldiers.

The fact is that the American view of terrorism is still geared to a law-and-order mind-set. The FBI knows damn well who the specific individuals are who killed Robert Stethem on TWA 847. But what is the FBI supposed to do, try to have the U.S. government get them extradited from Lebanon? The Minister of Justice in Lebanon is Nabih Berri, the very man who acted as ringmaster for the media event after Stethem was killed!

The FBI knows that the United States has the mechanism to pursue known terrorists. The United States doesn't need a massive response. It needs a surgical response, a special forces team. That team needs to be a covert and deniable group because it is not about to bring the killers of Robert Stethem out, à la Eichmann, and have a prolonged U.S. trial (during which other terrorists will take hostages to exchange for the prisoners). Even if convicted, the terrorists could hire that great appeals lawyer, who will see to it that after long delays the terrorists—who are "clearly mad"—will get sent to some peaceful institution like St. Elizabeth's, thus setting up that Washington psychiatric hospital for a terrorist hit.

In the case of an American special forces team going in, they would require some covert help from the CIA. To their disadvantage, the CIA is still recovering from the Church Committee's slaughter of its covert operations several years ago. This situation highlights further the need for the United States to coordinate its operations with other governments' intelligence mechanisms when its own sources have been damaged by Congressional action.

Brian Jenkins is one of the academic experts on terrorism who work for the Rand Corporation. I do not always agree with his analysis, but I heartily concur with his view that "We have lots of targets. We wring our hands, they don't. We worry about innocent bystanders. They have no such constraints."

Clearly it is up to the American leadership to demonstrate that rapid response teams such as relieved the hostage situations at Entebbe and Mogadishu and at the Iranian Embassy in London can be used elsewhere with the same favorable results. The terrorists calculate the American hesitancy as a weakness.

The media could play an educational role. Instead of giving the American public exclusively Rambo-style fiction, they could address American ignorance and fill the gaps. It was in that same *New York Times*/CBS poll I cited earlier that Americans were asked to name the countries they think of as responsible for terrorism. Less than a third named Libya. Only fifteen percent named the Soviet Union. Only nine percent named Iran. And only three percent named Syria. If you don't know who the enemy is, how can you begin to think about winning the war?

THIS IS NOT just an American problem. The mind-set of the rest of the world is at times, equally afflicted.

On December 18, 1985, the Security Council of the United Nations adopted a resolution that condemned "all acts of hostage-taking and abduction."

The vote was unanimous. The president of the Security Council, Léandre Bassole of Burkina Faso, an African state, was quoted as saying, "Never have I attended a Council meeting where unanimous agreement was reached in such a short time. It proves how urgently we need to solve the problem."

The Security Council called for the immediate, safe release of all hostages and abducted people.

Exactly nothing happened. Did anyone really believe that such an institution would be taken seriously by the terrorist world? It was another demonstration of impotence.

Perhaps the clue lies in what the U.N. Secretary General, Javier Pérez de Cuéllar, said just two months earlier: "We are living in another age of fanatics and we don't know what to do about it."

Wrong. The President of the United States *had* just done something about it by waylaying the plane carrying the *Achille Lauro* hijackers and forcing it to land in Italy, where the hijackers would be tried as criminals. He did so after Egypt had attempted to deceive the rest of the world as to the location of the hijackers of the *Achille Lauro* while conspiring to get the terrorists to a safe haven.

But the mind-set that enabled President Reagan in October 1985 to react in a way that was applauded by the world had softened by January 1986, when the United States did not immediately do anything about the post-Christmas outrages in Rome and Vienna on the grounds that there was no clear connection between Abu Nidal, perpetrator of the airport massacres, and specific targets. That misses the whole point. Nidal is a known terrorist leader who trains his terrorists in Libya. There is no "correct" time to get Nidal; he became a target of opportunity long ago. It is ridiculous to consider combating terrorism on a case by case basis. That is ducking the problem.

The training camp locations in Libya are known, just as are those in the Bekaa Valley in Lebanon, in Syria, Yemen, North Korea and elsewhere. The terrorists there are being trained with Soviet-made or Soviet-supplied weapons for missions against the West. All of the people in all of those training camps are either part of the terrorist instruction apparatus or volunteer terrorists in training. They are of a dozen different nationalities. A terrorist training camp is one place where if there are any innocent bystanders like the cook, he ought to get a job cooking elsewhere. If you feed a killer, you will die when he does.

Of course the same mind-set that sends an armada to relieve the hostages in the Teheran Embassy leads people to think of bombing and strafing. That's World War II thinking. The big-bang is the wrong approach to terrorism. The military has frequently been accused of preparing to fight the last war with better tools. The specialist must be employed—and to hell with the egos and the glory.

The Americans and Israelis have superb pilots. They operate highly sophisticated and extremely expensive flying machines. But the "if-you-have-them-use-them" philosophy is as absurd for these planes as for the Sixth Fleet. Their use is comforting and, as said before, retaliation brings satisfaction, but it is just a slap on the cheek. It is not coming to grips with the terrorists. Let's see those skilled pilots used to ferry in the small counterterrorist assault groups that can deal with terrorists the way the sergeant on *Hill Street Blues* urges his cops to deal with criminals: "Let's get them before they get us." I know and have seen the fear on the face of a terrorist when he suddenly realizes you are there, on his ground, and you have got him.

The war with the terrorists of the world is decidedly not a replay of World War II. The President doesn't need to worry that U.S. planes will be shot down by sophisticated Soviet anti-aircraft weaponry. He doesn't need expensive aircraft. He needs small counterterrorist teams of highly trained specialized personnel to take out the training camps in their accustomed fashion, quick in and quick out, with no time to start a slugging war. Send the strongest signal to the terrorist: "You are being hunted, nowhere is safe."

Can it be done? Absolutely. Without question.

Can things go wrong? Of course. As they can in any equation when you are dealing with violence. The experts are there to minimize that possibility. One irrevocable fact must be obvious to all—to lose the war against terrorism is incomprehensible. We were reminded of the terrifying consequences of a terrorist victory with the IRA bombing of the British Cabinet in Brighton. Had they succeeded, an already shaky world peace process would have wobbled like Jell-O. At that point, we are all vulnerable. You can't always rely on luck. When events get to this extreme, they have already gone too far. It is almost a case of too little and too late—unless the public and its leaders quickly develop an appropriate awareness.

PERHAPS, IN EXTREMIS, the required mind-set is portrayed in the Israeli example. They know that they are at war even between the outbreaks of conventional fighting every few years. They have had more people killed by terrorist action than any other. They now protect themselves in a different way than they used to because they have developed out of necessity a tougher mind-set. For instance, after they were plagued by car bombings, they established security zones in Southern Lebanon. Any resident wishing to enter the security zone with his vehicle has to have a license. They can't just drive up to an outpost of soldiers in their car. The resident of the security zone has to get out of his car several hundred feet from the guard post, walk toward the militiamen, identify himself, and show his license. If it checks out, the resident can then walk back to the car and drive it up to the post where it undergoes a search. *Anyone who violates this routine and drives up to guard post is shot on the spot.* This requires a tough mind-set. Yes, some of those shot were fools instead of knaves. But this security procedure has stopped at least two suicide car bombers. The number of victims of terrorism through car bombings has reduced dramatically. The Israelis were protecting their own, but interestingly enough, the majority of lives saved through these tough security procedures have been of Lebanese civilians since they constitute the

majority of victims in car bombings. The tough mind-set
policy has saved many lives and cost those of a few idiots
who weren't car bombers and didn't follow instructions.

The mind-set of the young and sometimes brainwashed
or duped suicide bombers is to kill other people. The mind-
set of the Israelis is to save themselves.

Similar conditions exist in Northern Ireland. The everyday movement of people is curtailed to an impossible
degree, the inconvenience adding hostility to an already
tense situation. Troops and police are continually alert,
tensed against the expected bullet in the back or the bomb
ambush.

Others in the West would do well to change their mind-
set before they are in the same position. The ultimate aim
of a tough mind-set is the prevention of further terrorism
and the protection of innocents.

TERRORISM IS SOMETIMES called "low intensity warfare," a
category that includes guerrilla actions. Lord Chalfont
has pointed out that the great advantage to our enemies of
low intensity warfare is that the payoff in strategic gain is
very great in relation to the expense. In addition, low
intensity warfare is conducted without the risk of confrontation with the full military force of, for instance, the United States. The point I want to emphasize is that U.S.
military force used conventionally is not productive.
When, in Lebanon, U.S. ships in the nearby Mediterranean lobbed expensive shells into the hills of Lebanon, it
wasn't accomplishing anything useful except perhaps
feeding the enemy some useful propaganda for their side
and fueling hatred, because shells fired from a distance in
such circumstances inevitably hit civilians as well as military targets. What is needed to deal with the terrorists'
"high geostrategic payoffs" are the counterterrorist forces
of the West.

Some of those forces have been capable of dealing with
terrorists effectively for years. Those that are not can be

readied quickly to the level of the SAS, GSG9, and Delta. These groups can be far more effective against known terrorists or terrorists-in-training than the terrorists are against us in their random murder of civilians. The people they kill are not fighters. Counterterrorists kill the enemy's fighters. Thus counterterrorist forces can quickly turn the tide of "high geo-strategic payoffs" also "without risk of confrontation on scale with the U.S. military force."

It takes will. It takes mind-set. And the clock is ticking.

SOME CIVILIANS I have encountered in my work think all that counterterrorists do is kill. Actually that is a small part of our work. A major part of our time is spent teaching *defensive* measures to government agencies in the West and to corporations whose facilities are threatened. We also teach the use of the highly technical equipment now available for protection. However, the ultimate use of the most skilled counterterrorists of the SAS, Delta, and GSG9 is in those instances when a terrorist outrage calls for a highly trained rapid response team to defuse the situation and eliminate the possibility of a long-drawn-out media event intended to destabilize society. A fireman fights fires most days of his life. A counterterrorist, you might say, spends most of his time in advanced training and training others, but when a terrorist fire breaks out, he and his colleagues are the specialists to call in to put that fire out by getting the arsonists and thus saving the lives of the trapped victims—and of future victims who would be caught in "fires" started by the same arsonists.

WHEN I THINK of the wrong mind-set about terrorism, I think of a female hostage and a male journalist.

The female hostage was in the Iranian Embassy in London when it was seized by terrorists. When the SAS swooped in on the terrorists, one of the terrorists lay down on the floor among the hostages. The female hostage shouted at the SAS man, "Don't shoot him, he's only a boy!" The SAS man could only think, "Does he have a gun? Is he wired with explosives?" and shot the terrorist dead.

"He's only a boy!" People sometimes forget that wars are always fought by boys of nineteen and twenty, commanded by older men. In Vietnam, aged twenty, I found there was no time to inquire about the enemy's age before killing him.

The male journalist is James Reston, widely syndicated political columnist of *The New York Times,* whose mind-set influences many. Immediately after President Reagan caused the Egyptian 737 with the *Achille Lauro* hijackers to be intercepted, Reston wrote, "The trouble with fanatics who hijack planes and ships, blow up embassies, murder diplomats and toss hand grenades like confetti into restaurants is that nobody knows who they are or who's in charge."

Mr. Reston, the readers of this book know. The perpetrators of the very act you were commenting on *were known, and action was taken against them.* Minds do not get reset while they are stuck, ostrichlike, in the sand.

The New York Times' lead editorial, the morning after the Rome and Vienna airport outrages, expressed its own outrage and concluded, "So the world is left frustrated, unable to do more than feel shock and revulsion. Yet that's precisely the right response. There's nothing more important at the moment than to let the shock and revulsion register, to nurture our sense of horror. Otherwise the terrorists win twice."

I wonder whether that some editorial writer would show support for action taken by a strong leadership, with all the risks involved.

I am not an historian, but I have participated in and witnessed crises in various parts of the world that will have a profound influence on history, whether in Vietnam, Rhodesia, or the Middle East. I have seen outrages committed in these theaters, often against helpless people,

which were known throughout Western society. But only
when such events are close to home does an editorial
appear. "So the world is left frustrated, unable to do more
than feel shock and horror." But the thought should not be
conveyed with negative undertones. The sense of horror
should be nurtured. There is nothing more important at the
moment than to let the shock and horror register. Then
take appropriate action fast.

I have regard for the *Times* and other distinguished
newspapers that have attempted to deal with terrorist and
hostage crises in their news columns fairly. It is the mind-
set when they editorialize that I am talking to. Please don't
tell us that our role is to be sitting ducks like the Marines in
Beirut. It is not characteristic of human nature to be beaten
in silence, to be passive when abused, humiliated, and
threatened with death. Our job is not to watch the West
being led by the nose by terrorism, to feel revulsion, and to
sit on our hands.

I have discussed the mind-set of the West with leaders
who sometimes did not know the full extent of my interest
and involvement. What I hear most often is that we are a
society of law, and they ask if it is really lawful to take
Special Forces action against terrorists unless it is to
relieve a hostage situation in which lives are being taken
or threatened. I am tempted to remind them that a state of
war exists in which the perpetrators have no respect for the
law or any fear of its penalties. In fact, the very bastions of
the legal profession have been penetrated and used by the
terrorists. In Europe, where nations as elsewhere think of
themselves as societies under law, lawyers have acted as
couriers for their terrorist clients and have also planned
prison escapes resulting in subsequent terrorist crime.
Lawyers have also been implicated in America at the time
of the Weathermen outrages. Martin Galvin of Noraid
enjoys the title of lawyer, yet openly supports IRA terrorists. I profoundly believe that lawyers and courts, by and

large, have been a deterrent to winning the war against terrorism and in some places have made such a mockery of justice as to make my blood boil.

Take the case of Brendan McFarlane and Gerard Kelly, who were serving sentences in Northern Ireland's Maze prison for murder and explosives offenses. In 1983 these two IRA killers were assisted in escaping from prison and spirited into Europe where they enjoyed two years of freedom before the Dutch police, in January, 1986, raided their flat in Amsterdam—which is one of the desirable places for IRA villains to escape to, another being New York. In both places they can successfully fight extradition requests because the mind-set of the law in both places is a sieve for criminals who pretend to be political refugees.

What was it the Dutch police found in the flat of those "political refugees" McFarlane and Kelly? They found arms, ammunition, fake IDs. Remember, these people had been jailed for murder, which for terrorists is as addictive as heroin is to the junkie. Was anyone thinking of further crimes they might yet commit—not to speak of lives already taken—when the fight to keep them from being extradited was played out in an Amsterdam courtroom?

The Irish lawyer opened his defense with the words, "I do not condone violence, but..." Sound familiar? Sitting in that courtroom, offering support, handshakes, contemptuous smiles to the enemy, was Gerry Adams, president of Sinn Fein. If Sinn Fein is a legitimate political party, what is its leader doing in court in support of convicted killers?

Also in support of the defense was Sean Macbride, winner of the Nobel Peace Prize and cofounder of Amnesty International. He was there as an expert witness. He said, "The activities of the IRA arose from an insurrectionary situation based on political discrimination."

I sympathize with the British officers who had to sit in the same courtroom with known terrorists and their supporters and listen to this unadultered nonsense. They must have been thinking: What the hell is the point of me hunting these bastards down in the first place.

Fortunately, the professionals involved in the war against terrorism see the IRA more realistically than do the Sean Macbrides of this world.

The escape of IRA terrorists from prison is a theme, not an incident. Just a few months earlier, on November 24, 1985, no fewer than eleven IRA prisoners tried to break out of jail in Belfast. Amongst these eleven were some of the top explosives experts of the IRA. Would a court hold that explosives are a legitimate means of political expression? Among the eleven was Thomas McMahon, the convicted murderer of Earl Mountbatten. Would a court hold that murder is a legitimate means of political expression? Also among the eleven was Martin Ferris, the leader of the 1984 attempt to smuggle arms from the United States into Ireland on board the trawler *Marita Ann.* Would a court hold that smuggling arms is a legitimate means of political expression? You can see what the war against terrorism is up against when it faces the mind-set of lawyers who work not for justice and to protect the innocent victims but to exploit the loopholes in the law.

How did the eleven expect to escape? First, a gun was smuggled into the prison. So were explosives. The prisoners held their guards at gunpoint, then made their way through a series of gates with the help of duplicated keys. Their intention was to get through the main gates with the use of the explosives. As it turned out, the explosives were insufficient and failed to breach the main gates. If their breakout plan had worked, would the eleven have used the night run of an Irish fishing trawler out of Galway Bay, slipping close by the Isle of Aran, and out into the Atlantic to rendezvous with Basque ETA friends amongst the Spanish fishing fleet, to be spirited safely ashore near the Spanish town of San Sebastian?

These terrorists were not attempting to escape in order to take up early retirement. Their escape was organized because their expertise was needed for the joint offensive planned by certain elements of the European terrorist community.

Actually not all of them would be needed for the offensive. Some of these "heroes" might have surfaced in the United States for fund-raising propaganda purposes in the full knowledge that they had the protection of the anti-extradition sentiment of the American courts. If laws prohibit essentially defensive actions against terrorists in law-abiding societies, those laws need to be altered. It is no wonder that the intelligence agencies are frequently forced to ignore the law and carry out deniable operations with the tacit understanding of the lawmakers.

WHERE DID SINN Fein President Gerry Adams next surface after the travesty in Amsterdam? On March 22, 1986 he was on the Dublin courthouse steps to embrace a terrorist with a face that was familiar to me. Her name is Evelyn Glenholmes. Her reception committee included Sinn Fein's former publicity director, Danny Morrison, and Londonderry's Sinn Fein leader, Martin McGuinness. Terrorist Glenholmes had been released on a thin technicality.

This 29-year-old heroine of Sinn Fein was wanted for no less than three murders, one attempted murder, and various arms and explosive offenses. According to the warrants, this lass, released by the judge in Dublin, was involved in the following:

1. The horrifying bomb explosion outside the Chelsea army barracks. This bomb was packed with six-inch nails that killed two people and maimed no less than 37 others in the heart of London.

2. The murder of Kenneth Howarth, a bomb disposal expert who was killed while bravely trying to disarm a bomb planted in a hamburger restaurant in London's busy Oxford Street.

3. The attempted murder of Sir Stewart Pringle, the Commandant General of the Royal Marines, by way of a

car bomb outside his London home. He lost a leg but didn't die as planned.

4. A bomb attack on the home of the United Kingdom Attorney General, Sir Michael Havers.

5. "Minor" offenses like stashing explosives, firearms, and ammunition at a farm in Oxfordshire, England, between August 1981 and October 1983.

Within an hour of the time that this much-wanted terrorist, Evelyn Glenholmes, was spotted, arrested, and detained at Dublin's Mountjoy Prison, her lawyer was in the High Court claiming that she was being illegally detained. She had gotten through the sieve of the law before, but this time around there was a barely two-week-old agreement between Dublin and Northern Ireland, and Ireland had signed the European Convention for the suppression of terrorism. This time, I prayed, the mind-set of the law would have changed and she wouldn't be let go. She was, on the grounds that the warrants for her arrest were faulty.

Back in 1982 I had a bit of an encounter with Evelyn Glenholmes and her comrades in arms.

I was well into an operation on behalf of Spain, tracking down ETA leaders in their sanctuary in the south of France, close to the Spanish border. During one of my frequent debriefings with my Spanish contacts, they expressed their concern with regard to intelligence they had picked up about an IRA arms shipment. At the time there was a free flow of favors between the IRA, who lent the Spanish terrorists instructors in bomb-making and Eastern bloc weaponry in exchange for ETA assistance in obtaining a massive supply of explosives and arms.

A sizeable arms shipment was being moved out of Greece on a coal boat purchased and crewed by IRA members, one of whom was Evelyn Glenholmes. The ship had been tracked through the Mediterranean and the Strait of Gibraltar and up the Portuguese coast to the Spanish port of San Sebastian. The arms were unloaded and transferred to a truck for hauling across Europe to a ferry port, where the truck would complete its journey to

Ireland by water. Meanwhile, with the hope of taking the
attention of intelligence off the truck, the ship continued to
Ireland as scheduled with its manifested cargo of scrap
iron.

Our operation was well underway in Southern France,
bordering Spain, and during one of the frequent debriefings with my Spanish contacts their concern for the IRA
arms shipment was again discussed. By that time the
truck was traveling across the country to join the main A6
autoroute toward Paris. The Irish terrorists had now been
joined by a Spanish driver and additional Spanish support
in a following car. We agreed with our Spanish client to
dispatch some of our team who were operating out of Mar-
seilles to intercept the truck south of Avignon and keep it
under surveillance.

My team consisted of four ex-Foreign Legionnaires,all
very qualified for the intercept operation and in taking
care of themselves. The Spanish clearly conveyed that
they wanted the truck stopped at all cost, but wanted to
liaise further with the British authorities before giving the
order to go in. Two hours after this briefing the terrorists
were sitting at separate tables in a motorway service area
restaurant blending in with the traveling public. The
Spanish bodyguard group was carefully not making open
contact with the truck party. Also sitting a few tables away
were two of my men, looking like ordinary Frenchmen,
their fitness and weapons hidden under their loose jackets.
The third member of my team was outside watching the
truck, while the fourth was describing to me from a public
telephone the terrorist Evelyn Glenholmes, who was sitting only three tables away from him. His experienced eye
had also detected the presence of other, more official, surveillance of the same group. He was convinced that the
official watchers were unaware of the Spanish back-up
group, who he had determined were heavily armed. He also
saw indications that the terrorists were planning to split
up. He sought permission from me to sabotage the truck in
such a way as to reduce it to scrap and, at a selected

location down the road, to isolate the Spanish group and effect their deaths.

The four principal members of the terrorist group were known targeted terrorists, and the rest of the party were certainly not just along for the ride. It was as good an opportunity as ever to carry out a very effective job of prevention, but this was not to be.

My Spanish contact, with some degree of resignation, advised me that the British had an operation under way and my team should be called off. When my man called me again after thirty, somewhat apprehensive, minutes I detected a note of disappointment and some anger in his voice as I passed on this order to back off. He later reported that they had followed the terrorists for another two hours and had observed them split up. A car collected Glenholmes and took her in the direction of Geneva, while the truck continued on its way, and the Spaniards turned for home.

The eventual outcome was that the arms reached Northern Ireland and among them were two M60 heavy machine guns, similar to the type used to gun down Captain Westmacott. As for Glenholmes, we observe her entering a courtroom more than three years later, protected by legal procedure, as is her murdering brother-in-arms Brendon McFarlane, simultaneously fighting extradition from Amsterdam.

The shocking fact is that in the interim too many brave servicemen have died, innocent bystanders have been killed and maimed in Ireland, and the British cabinet was almost wiped out.

ISRAEL, I HAVE said, has had to deal with active terrorism more than any other nation in our time. Like other nations, it is torn by controversy over retaliation and prevention. Israel is home to many mind-sets. Yet, early in January 1986, Brigadier General Gideon Machanaimi, a national security adviser to the Israeli prime minister, said after the attacks at the Rome and Vienna airports, "The best way, or let's say the successful way, to combat terrorism" is to assassinate terrorist leaders.

General Machanaimi stated the obvious when he said, "Once one of the leaders has been assassinated, we found a long period of peace in the area."

TO PUT IT as succinctly as possible, the wrong mind-set is "free the hostages at any price."

The right mind-set is "kill the terrorists and prevent the hostages from being taken in the first place."

Perhaps the West can learn a lesson from the East. When Anatoly Shcharansky, the well-known Soviet dissident, was released after nearly nine years' imprisonment in the Soviet Union, he was allowed to fly to Israel where he continued his outspoken ways against the Soviet regime. When people with the wrong mind-set nervously wondered aloud in his presence whether his outspokenness would damage the chances of his mother and brother getting out of the Soviet Union, Shcharansky was quick to say something along the lines of *My good behavior won't get my relatives out. If I keep telling the truth I might get them out*. Nine years in Gulag had reinforced his mind-set as to what works and what doesn't.

WHEN I HAVE discussed the mind-set of the West with other professionals in the counterterrorist field, their impatience, like mine, shows. But as deniable people or restricted by security, my colleagues cannot publicly broadcast the realities or use the more efficient means of the media to reveal the present inadequacies in the fight against terrorism. If they did they would be met with cries from media and politicians alike—"The public doesn't want to hear about that, it's too strong." So the public remains ignorant of the real dangers and of the reassurance from its leaders that the capabilities exist to defeat terrorism now.

10

Appeasement

I am going to give short shrift to the idea that terrorists can be appeased. History has repeatedly shown that you cannot bargain with tyranny. However, nearly half a century after Neville Chamberlain, the then British prime minister, tried to appease Hitler in order to achieve "peace in our time," there are, in fact, influential people in the U.S., British, and European governments and media who advocate appeasement though they cannot demonstrate a single instance in which it has worked against terrorists.

It is not difficult to set before you a few of the many examples where appeasement has failed.

In August 1981, President François Mitterand of France—a country that should know that appeasement doesn't work—released two imprisoned terrorist leaders, Jean Marc Rouillan and Natalie Menigon, after they'd spent less than a year in jail. That resulted in the formation of Action Directe, France's most active terrorist group. Rouillan used hit-and-run tactics against French, U.S., and Jewish targets. He inspired others. The killing intensified. In 1982, he regrouped the terrorist underground, linking up with Palestinians, the IRA, and ETA.

As I have indicated, our operation against the Basque ETA terrorist leaders *in France* was a direct result of the French turning a blind eye to terrorists using France as a refuge. Carlos, perhaps the best-known terrorist leader before Abu Nidal, used to float in and out of Paris with impunity. The German Red Army Faction and the Italian Red Brigades, Israelis, Latin Americans, Arabs, Iranians, and Armenians bent on terrorist acts have all used France as a base because they felt relatively safe there.

Mitterand not only gave a gift of amnesty to thirty-one *convicted* terrorists but announced that he was going to eliminate the State Security Court, which has jurisdiction over terrorist offenses. World terrorism couldn't have received a nicer present.

Mitterand's appeasement proved just as counterproductive as Neville Chamberlain's. On January 25, 1985, General René Audron, head of arms sales for the Ministry of Defense, was shot down. More terrorist activity followed. On December 7, 1985, yet another campaign of random terror began in France, directed at its most crowded commercial areas. One bomb, wrapped in a Kuwaiti newspaper, was left in a famous Parisian department store, Au Printemps, by two dark-complected men spotted by a saleswoman in the crowded store just before the bomb exploded. That same day, in the nearby Galeries Lafayette department store, an explosive Christmas present ruined Christmas for thirty-five families whose members were maimed when the bomb went off.

The reaction to Mitterand's appeasement policy accelerated in February 1986. On the 3rd, an explosion rocked a Champs-Elysées shopping arcade, crowded with moviegoers, strollers, and window-shoppers, many of them foreign tourists. Smoke from the explosion filled the Hotel Claridge above the arcade. Eight people were hurt, three seriously. Pedestrians fled in panic. The police had trouble reaching the wounded because the explosion set off the automatic sprinkler system, flooding the arcade area. A group calling itself the Committee of Solidarity with Arab and Middle Eastern Political Prisoners took credit, demanding the release from prison of three terrorists who had not yet been given amnesty. One of them is Anis Naccache, who headed the Iranian team working for the Ayotollah Khomeini that tried to assassinate the former prime minister, Shapur Bakhtiar. The second whose release was demanded was George Ibrahim Abdallah of the Lebanese Armed Revolutionary Faction. The third was the leader of an Armenian terrorist gang that killed seven people in a bomb attack at Orly airport. Iranian, Lebanese, Armenian—the solidarity is not of nationality but of terrorism.

The same day as the Champs-Elysées shopping arcade outrage, the French police got lucky and defused a bomb on the Eiffel Tower before it exploded. The following day, February 4, 1986, the French police were not so lucky. A terrorist bomb exploded in a bookstore on the Place Saint-Michel. The next day's Paris bomb went off at the Forum des Halles. The next day, February 6, marked a milestone: there were 80 bomb scares in a single day in Paris. Parisians had begun to see bombs everywhere. The terrorists had succeeded in their primary mission of destabilizing the people of the French capital. Their message was loud as well as clear.

Yet there was still something missing from the terrorist successes in Paris: death. This they finally achieved on the last day of winter, March 20, 1986. It was an important day in France. A new prime minister, the former Mayor of Paris Jacques Chirac, had just taken office. A *Paris-Match* photographer, Patrick Bruchet, had just come back from the Elysée Palace where he had recorded the change of government for his magazine and posterity. Bruchet was standing right in front of an arcade of expensive boutiques on the main street of France, the Champs-Elysées, when a much more powerful bomb than the one that rocked the Claridge Hotel went off, sending bleeding shoppers streaming from the arcade. Two did not make it. The Arab terrorists who claimed credit for the bomb finally had the deaths they had wanted. That twenty-eight other people were wounded in the explosion was merely a bonus.

And so the first port of call of the new French prime minister was a scene of terrorist destruction. One of his lieutenants was heard to say, "The Champs-Elysées is a symbol of Paris and a symbol of France. The fight against terrorism must be a priority." At a press conference later, the new prime minister said, "I am horrified by the animal character and inhumanity of these attacks." He cried out for an "important reinforcement of coordination of efforts of the democratic nations that are the victims of these acts," which is exactly what I am arguing for in this book in specific detail.

The French have a talent for rhetoric. They also have a talent for appeasement.

While the six previous attacks since early December 1985, were making the French capitol a nerve-wracking place for its denizens as well as tourists, the French were doing their best to block an American proposal, accepted by several democracies, to discuss a joint effort to respond to terrorist attacks in the future. France was said to be concerned that any concerted effort against Libya, for instance, would produce what the French called "an Arab front" unfriendly to the West. Do the French think the Arab front is currently friendly to the West? Or is France, despite the daily terrorist attacks, still biting the wormy apple of appeasement?

WHEN TWA FLIGHT 847 was hijacked in June 1985 and American seaman Robert Dean Stethem killed, President Reagan pledged that the terrorists responsible would be brought to justice. In July warrants were issued for the arrest of Mohammed Hammadei, Ali Atwa, and Hassan Izz-al-Din. Conspicuous by its absence—the court documents were sealed at the time—was the name of the man

characterized as "the brain of the TWA hijacking," a Lebanese Shiite named Imad Mughniyah. The Americans
had a special interest in Mughniyah because he had also
been implicated in the car and truck bombings of the
French and American barracks in Beirut, with 241
Marines dead in the latter attack alone. Officials have
linked Mughniyah to Abu Nidal, who was responsible for
the Rome and Vienna airport attacks after Christmas
1985. Clearly Imad Mughniyah is a terrorist leader of great
importance. The Americans wanted him very badly.

Late in 1985, U.S. intelligence sources received information that Mughniyah was planning to go to France. The
Americans tipped off their French counterparts. With good
fortune on their side, the French spotted Mughniyah and
then let him go. The Americans were dismayed by this
clear attempt by the French to appease the terrorists in the
hope that they might get their hostages in Lebanon
released. Of course, the appeasement didn't work. Moreover, the French have continued their very strong opposition to extraditing terrorist fugitives to the United States
on the grounds that Americans have refused to extradite to
Britain wanted IRA members caught in the United States.
Meanwhile, Vice President Bush's task force on combat-
ting terrorism was preparing its report, which specified,
"Without a viable, comprehensive cooperative effort, terrorism and its supporters will benefit from the uncoordinated actions of its victims."

As the French say, *Plus ça change, plus c'est la même
chose.* The more things change, the more they remain the
same.

ISRAEL, A CONSTANT target of Arab terrorism, has been led
from time to time by political considerations to swap terrorist murderers for Israeli nationals in terrorist hands.
Usually, the numbers are canted very highly in favor of
the Arabs. This satisfies a domestic argument that one
Israeli is worth any number of Arabs. Can such appease-

ment be characterized as having "humanitarian" motives, the release of Israeli prisoners? Only if it can be shown that the released terrorists and convicted murderers have been so affected that they will commit no further crimes of terror. That is patently not so. How many times must the world watch freed terrorists belligerently making the "V for Victory" sign? Must we listen to their threats against their recent captors to realize that releasing known killers is an antihumanitarian act because it will inevitably result in further killings of innocents?

Austria was the first Western country to officially recognize the PLO. It did so in 1979 under the leadership of Chancellor Bruno Kreisky, a Jew in a German-speaking country. Austria's pro-Arab position caused a lot of embarrassment when terrorists picked the Vienna airport as one of their two targets for the December 27, 1985, outrages.

Austria has a relatively large Arab population that moves about without any considerable surveillance by the police. So has Italy. It is no coincidence that Austria and Italy were chosen as the two target areas for the December 27 massacres. If you create such an environment and allow terrorist factions with varying loyalties to flow in and out of your country with ease in an attempt to placate them, you are setting yourself up to reap the whirlwind.

An amazing public example of recent appeasement was in the wake of the hijacking of the Italian cruise ship, *Achille Lauro.*

Libya's role in the hijacking was well known. The hijacking was planned by Abu Nidal, whose safe haven is Libya. Libya's Qaddafi is an implacable enemy of Egypt.

When the ship was retrieved from the hijackers, four gunmen were said to be in the hands of the Egyptians. But were there only four? The passengers, herded together, were guarded by four armed men with walkie-talkies. These were later identified by Italian authorities as Hallah Abdullah al-Hassan, age 19; Majed Youssef al-Molky, age 23; Abdel Atif Ibrahim, age 20; and Hammad Ali Abdullah, age 29. According to eyewitnesses, these men some-times seemed to be using their walkie-talkies to communi-cate not with each other but with someone not present. Judge Stanley L. Kubacki, of the Philadelphia Common Pleas Court, a hostage aboard the *Achille Lauro,* told the FBI after his release that he and his wife Sophia, also a hostage, were "absolutely certain" there had been six hijackers, not four. Judge Kubacki and his wife said that, in addition to the four hijackers guarding the passengers, they believed there were at least two others, one on the bridge to control the ship's movements and one in the engine room to insure that orders from the bridge were carried out. Judge and Mrs. Kubacki also told the FBI that when the *Achille Lauro* hijacking was almost over, two men not seen earlier came into the lounge where the hos-tages were kept and spoke to the four hijackers who had been guarding them.

Judge Kubacki, 70, has had long experience observing detail. It was he, for instance, who noted that two shots were fired on the starboard side of the ship at exactly 11:10 A.M. the morning Leon Klinghoffer was killed. Judge Kubacki's observations included the fact that one of the two men who joined the four gunmen in the lounge was tall, slender, and wore a silky grayish-blue shirt. Was that Mohammed Abbas who, the United States said, had led the hijack expedition?

After the hostages were released on shore in Egypt, Pres-ident Hosni Mubarak lied to both the press and the Ameri-can government about the hijackers' presence in Egypt, claiming they had left Egypt when in fact they had not.

Mubarak was appeasing his archenemy Qaddafi. He was also secretly negotiating for at least ten hours with President Bourguiba of Tunisia to accept the "return" of the hijackers, who had carried stolen Tunisian passports.

The Reagan administration put pressure on Tunisia to refuse safe haven to the terrorists. Tunisia's Bourguiba was said to be influenced more by the threat of an Israeli bombing raid than by the American president's pressure. The Tunisians closed their air space.

That's when President Reagan and American Defense Secretary Caspar Weinberger planned a bold move to intercept the plane carrying the *Achille Lauro* hijackers. But they nearly jeopardized that move by talking to each other *on an open line.* A White House official later said Reagan and Weinberger decided against using a secure line because time was of the essence and *their coding machines were not compatible without time-consuming adjustments.* One has to ask if their conversation was not about the *Achille Lauro* hijackers but about a Soviet-generated emergency, would time also have been of the essence and would they have made their counterplans on an open line? I think the Americans had better get their secret communications apparatuses in order and compatible with today's emergencies!

In any event, one of America's numerous ham radio operators—this one was in Chicago—picked up Reagan and Weinberger's open-line conversation, told his brother about it, and the brother called CBS News in New York to spread the word. The security consciousness of Americans from the president on down to ham radio operators needs some rethinking.

In the end, Bouguiba double-crossed Mubarak by cooperating with the Americans. President Reagan ordered U.S. planes to intercept the Egyptair 737 carrying the hijackers. This was a far more difficult operation than most civilians realize. It required two U.S. Navy versions of the AWACS plane to track the many simultaneous Mediterranean flights and isolate the one plane being looked for. This was made easier by learning through radio intercepts what the flight's transponder code was. The flight then appeared as an enlarged dot on the radar screens inside the prowling AWACS, allowing them to vector the interceptors to the airliner. There were six flights of F-14s. The mission had to be done at night. They had very little time. It involved the tricky use of air-to-air refueling to keep the planes aloft. Yet it was successful.

The Egyptair 737 was forced down to a joint Italian-NATO base in Sigonella in Sicily. Aboard were not only the four gunmen who guarded the passengers, but also a real catch: Mohammed Abbas, leader of the expedition, and a Palestine Liberation Front official whose identity remained mysterious in press reports. There should be no mystery about this second leader. He was Ozzudin Badrak Kan, who heads Mohammed Abbas's *military* branch. Is it possible that these were the other two men Judge Kubacki and his wife had seen whispering to the four gunmen?

Prime Minister Craxi of Italy assured President Reagan by phone on the night of October 10th that he would hold Abbas and the others to give the Americans a chance to begin extradition proceedings.

But Craxi chickened out. He opted for appeasement, and let Abbas and Kan escape arrest. Only after they had boarded a Yugoslav airliner for Belgrade and were safely out of reach did Craxi do an about face and try to appease the Americans by issuing a warrant for Abbas's arrest. The U.S. Ambassador to Italy, Maxwell M. Rabb, said the release of Abbas was "incomprehensible to the United States." Craxi's excuse? He thought letting the master terrorist go was necessary to avert a collapse of Italy's ties with the Arab world. The Yugoslavs, of course, let Abbas escape the wrath of the Americans and disappear into a safe haven.

Meanwhile Farouk Kaddoumi, who heads the Political Department of the PLO, was trying to convince the United Nations Security Council in New York that Leon Klinghoffer might have died of natural causes. When Klinghoffer's body washed up on shore, an autopsy revealed the two bullet wounds that killed him—not exactly "natural causes."

The day before PLO official Kaddoumi addressed the United Nations, Yasir Arafat, head of the PLO, at a press conference in Tunis was asking Egypt to hand over the "four" hijackers of the *Achille Lauro*. His "good guy/bad guy" strategy was again in evidence. With the hijacking terminated, he was turning on the "good guy" spigot. He said he had sent Mohammed Abul Abbas and Hani al-Hassan to Egypt while the *Achille Lauro* was still at sea to be part of a joint Egyptian-Italian-Palestinian negotiating team. At least he was telling the world that terrorist leader Abbas was his man. The question, of course, is, was his man part of a "negotiating team" that went to Egypt after the fact—then joined the triumphant hijackers in the Egyptair 737 that was intercepted—or was Abbas, as the Americans claimed, the mastermind of the hijacking itself?

In any event, the intercept of the getaway plane put the worldwide terrorist community on notice. One optimistic Congressman, David Drier of California, said, "For years Americans have had to count the days of a capitulation to terrorism. Let today [the day of the intercept] mark Day One of our response to terrorism." Perhaps we should cynically ask where Congressman Drier has been for the last ten years of terrorist activity.

The Egyptair's plane being forced down on Italian territory was characterized in *The New York Times* as "the first overt act against terrorism by an American President since the disaster at Desert One in Iran."

Mubarak's attempt at appeasement of the more bellicose members of the Arab community by sneakily trying to get terrorist killers home scot-free didn't work, to Egypt's intense embarrassment and moral shame. Ironically, by not succeeding, Mubarak lost face with those terrorist factions he was coerced to help.

It is highly significant that Moscow, which funds and supports a majority of terrorist organizations, reacted favorably to the American use of force in intercepting the hijackers' plane. This is the opposite of what appeasers expect. The official Soviet press agency, Tass, said, "The

Americans' anger at the hijackers' crime aboard a cruise liner is understandable and just. The crimes of terrorists, no matter where they are committed, must be punished most severely. And severity must be shown unfailingly to all perpetrators of such crimes."

The impact of that statement could not be lost. Just as when President Kennedy stood toe-to-toe with Khrushchev during the Soviet missile crisis in Cuba and the Soviets backed down, here was an example of an American president reacting properly to a terrorist act, being applauded by the mother of terrorist countries.

At this same time, three Soviet diplomats were being held captive in Beirut by a Moslem sect trying to force the Soviet Union to put pressure on its client state Syria to end the fighting in Tripoli. The Moslem had already murdered one Soviet national and dumped his body in the streets of Beirut. The terrorist ritual is: kill at least one to show you mean business.

The Soviets mean business, too. They kidnapped a number of Lebanese, cut off parts of their bodies and sent them to Moslem militia leaders. The three Russian hostages were quickly let go.

The Soviets learned that even they are not beyond the reach of the terrorists; it was possible for their own ox to be gored, and they didn't like it. Their response was tough. This seizing of Soviet hostages no doubt influenced the Soviet press releases and led to praise of an American *military* act. On a previous occasion when the Soviets were helped by the Americans to free Soviet hostages held by guerrillas in Burma, the event went unreported. The change did not go unnoticed in the counterterrorist forces of several nations.

Cairo is about one hundred miles upriver (south) in the Nile Delta, about the same distance from the two port cities of Alexandria and Port Said. The *Achille Lauro* sailed east from Alexandria on the night of Monday, October 7, 1985. Some of the passengers were safely off the ship, exploring

the pyramids and planning to catch up with the cruise in
Port Said. They missed the hijacking, for it was Monday
night when the ship was seized. The ship was made to sail
northeast to Tartus, a Syrian port just north of the
Lebanon. Apparently the Syrians decided not to get
involved. The ship was turned away, and it headed west
toward Cyprus on Tuesday, but before reaching Cyprus
turned south to Egypt again. The hijackers surrendered
the ship at Port Said on Thursday, October 10.

During this nightmare journey, the hostages aboard the
ship were terrified for their lives, particularly the Americans whom the hijackers had separated from the other
passengers and moved about the ship as a group. One of
the terrorists, "a short young fellow" according to an eye-
witness, "seemed to really have it in for the Americans. He
kept browbeating us and threatening us."

President Reagan wasn't sitting on his hands. Before
the surrender agreement was reached, Reagan had ordered American counterterrorist forces moved into place
for an assault. The Navy Seals—they are trained for sea,
air, and land operations, hence their name—were to take
the lead. The equipment they had available included small
boats especially useful in a night attack, rocket-powered
grappling hooks, and rubber-encased ladders for silent
boarding. (They also had a catapult that can throw a man
safely several stories high, though some of the people I
know and I would have been disinclined to use that technique. The ideal attack on a ship like the *Achille Lauro*
would have employed five three-man teams, and that's not
a catapult operation.)

A point to keep in mind is that a civilian ship doesn't
have electronic warfare warning equipment. Its radar is of
the kind that would have made it possible to tail the ship
and approach very close without anybody on board being
the wiser. It's no secret that the Americans have tested the
use of helicopters during driving rainstorms and have
been able to get them over the stern of a ship without the
captain or anyone else on the bridge knowing about it.

In the event, the plans for the assault were hushed up as soon as the hijackers were on their way in to Port Said to surrender. The chance for the United States to prove its counterterrorist capability would await another day, and then it would take a different form—intercepting the jet taking the perpetrators to freedom.

Taking the ship would have had a good chance of success. Not too many years ago, I was part of a small group made up mainly of U.S. Navy Seal Team antiterrorist specialists who "captured" an oil rig off the Texas coast. The men on the oil rig had no idea we were coming. When we showed up, they thought we were real terrorists. The point of the exercise, of course, was to demonstrate the vulnerability of oil platforms to terrorist attack, but there are some similarities between a ship and an oil rig out in the water.

Relieving a hijacked ship is a bit more difficult. While the Americans had communicated secretly with the Italians about their planned assault on the *Achille Lauro,* it was not to be an international operation, which is what I favor and which would have been particularly appropriate in this instance because an international effort would have had the advantage of the Italian frogmen, who are among the best in the world. In fact, in any contribution of counterterrorist resources to an international operation, the Italian frogmen would make a significant contribution.

Many people have canceled their plans to take a cruise since the *Achille Lauro* affair, which is a pity since cruising the Mediterranean is a once-in-a-lifetime experience. Perhaps the reader will feel more comfortable about taking a cruise ship if he knows in precise detail what an international counterterrorist group can accomplish in such circumstances.

Before launching an attack, we would have had intelligence information from several sources. Though we couldn't count on the captain the way we can on the captain of an airliner, we could find out what was going on on the ship by means of submarine surveillance (the West has plenty of submarines in the Mediterranean). In addition, plans of the ship would be made available.

The actual attack would have been made at night. Each team would have a preplanned route over the decks or through the ship's narrow gangways to the known location of the terrorists. This assault from start to finish would be carried out silently and rapidly. The teams, using silenced weapons, knives, and bare-handed techniques against any opposition, would stealthily converge on the hostage position. Any stray passengers or crew would be locked in a convenient cabin as each section was cleared, and any terrorists encountered would be killed instantly. All this would be achieved in a perfected, no-nonsense manner.

Having gained access to the ship, the team would remain concealed until a "go" signal was received from its support group lying out in the water in the darkness, observing the terrorists' movements through night-vision goggles. They will be coordinating with tactical headquarters, known as TACGROUP, via a submarine or aircraft communications link. TACGROUP would meanwhile have been maintaining a continuous radio watch on the ship, monitoring communications to and from the terrorists. It is the analyses from these communications and observations from the support group that dictate the timing of the "go" signal. The tactical, safety, and urgency assessment would be updated by the minute. A countdown atmosphere not dissimilar to a NASA launch prevails.

The team, including a support group of three men, would have been assembled, probably at an air base in Sicily, and air-transported to the target area.

Onward penetration of the target area would be achieved in one of two ways. Ideally, an Allied submarine would be in the area. The team would carry out a HALO parachute jump, exiting the aircraft at a very high altitude, perhaps as high as 25,000 feet, depending on factors such as wind, weather, and the state of the sea. The people on the ship would be totally unaware of this. The team would jump already kitted-up for the assault and would be wearing breathing apparatus that would allow them to dive down to the submarine. The submarine would not surface throughout the duration of the operation. Rendezvousing with the submarine is achieved by release from the submarine of a floating buoy attached to a strong line. The buoy is small but designed in such a way as to assist the swimmers in finding it. In some cases the team, after they have descended into the water and discarded their parachutes, would form up around the leader. Equipped with a hand-portable direction-finding device, they would swim to the rendezvous, tracking in on the DF signal from the buoy. On reaching the buoy, their breathing gear already on, they would descend down the line, entering the submarine through its flooded chambers. The submarine would then proceed at full running speed to the target.

On reaching the proximity of the ship, the team would exit from the submarine via the flooded hatches. Once on the surface, they would carry out a combat swim to the ship. The support group would simultaneously swim off at a tangent to set up surveillance. Semisubmersible inflatables can be used to assist the swim and the carrying of equipment. The use of a submarine would depend on one being coincidentally positioned within an acceptable running time to the target ship. Should this not be the case, the team would have to carry out a more hazardous HALO drop closer to the ship with less equipment and would have an exhausting swim to the target. Either way the assault team has been assembled, equipped, and transported from Europe to the Mediterranean target in a matter of hours.

In a coordinated attack, the five teams would clamber aboard at the stern of the vessel using suction ascenders, a magnetic device that allows one team member to pull himself up the hull and then drop climbing ropes for the others.

An alternative boarding method from the sea would be to shoot explosive grappline bolts into the upper superstructure with climbing lines attached. This has the risk of noise and malfunction. Actual entry would be through the galley loading door, through selected portholes or over a lower deck, taking out any sentry targeted by the support group and relayed to the assault team through a radio link or Morse signal. The last phase of the assault would then begin, activated by the order "go."

All fifteen of us would have assigned objectives, the main priority being to get the terrorists. One team would secure the bridge and take control of the public address system, this to be used to contain the passengers and suppress their panic after the shooting stopped. They would also prevent the terrorist on the bridge—who at this point would be diverted by conversation on the radio—from shouting a warning to his brothers in arms.

During the assault, the team leader would keep track of his teams by clipped running commentary through a fully duplex radio system. This system has voice-activated microphones that are attached around the throat, which means you can talk without taking your hands away from your weapons.

On reaching the hostage location, the fact that you are on a ship becomes insignificant. You are faced with a room full of hostages under the eyes of terrorist guards.

In seconds, you locate the terrorists, assess your fields of fire, and individual targets are delegated. You have surprise on your side and you go in like a steamroller, with the clear intent of putting a killing shot, followed at once by a second to make sure, into your targeted terrorist.

It is very difficult for terrorists to control an area as large as a passenger liner. There are too many decks, too many places to hide, too many square feet of space. And too many hostages for a small number of terrorists to deal with. In the case of the *Achille Lauro,* the four terrorists used maximum threats to herd the passengers into confined areas, making them controllable. When they attacked, they made seizure of the captain of the ship their top priority, knowing that the laws of international shipping permit only one hand weapon to be carried on board, which is to remain in the captain's control.

There has been a lot of puzzlement about *why* the *Achille Lauro* was hijacked. Why would terrorists pick a big ship full of passengers instead of an airplane? Why did they agree to surrender in less than three days' time?

We have to backtrack to pick up some facts. The reputed organizer of the operation was Mohammed Abul Abbas, who as recently as November 29, 1984, was elected to Yasir Arafat's eleven-member executive committee. Earlier in 1984, the PLO splintered into pro-Arafat and pro-Syrian factions, and one of its offshoots, the Palestine Liberation Front, split into no less than three separate factions. One of the factions aligned itself with an anti-Arafat guerrilla group led by Abu Musa. Another, led by Abdul Fitah Ghanem, elected to take Syria as its base of operations. The third faction, headed by Mohammed Abul Abbas, pledged its loyalty to Arafat, and it was in gratitude that Arafat chose Abbas for his executive committee.

Next, let us also remember that just a week before the hijacking of the *Achille Lauro* the Israelis bombed the PLO headquarters in Tunis. The PLO wanted to send a message to Israel: "If you can reach out 1,500 miles to strike at us, we can reach out 1,500 miles to strike back at you." According to Arab sources in Beirut and Nicosia, the planned target was Ashdod, a port in Israel, to be attacked *by sea*. The fact is that by late 1985 the Israelis had sealed all of their land borders pretty well, and so one option open to the Palestinians was an attack from the Mediterranean on Israel's long coastline. At least one of the *Achille Lauro* hijackers *had been on an earlier cruise* of the same ship to study it and to case the layout in Ashdod, one of its ports of call. When the decision was made to avenge the Israeli raid on Tunis, the go ahead signal was given to Mohammed Abbas's team.

They boarded the cruise ship as passengers in Genoa. It was each enough for them to smuggle on board their machine guns, hand grenades, explosives, and other necessaries.

The ship set sail for Alexandria. Most of the passengers were, like on most cruise ships, older people. The four Arabs who were in public view were conspicuous because of their youth and complexions and how they spoke. Some of the passengers got suspicious when the oldest of the four, named Abdullah, was paged again and again over the ship's intercom system by the others. An Israeli couple named Pracher reported their suspicions to a member of the crew. This might have been dismissed since Israelis might be considered to be hypersensitive, but other passengers also had suspicions and reported them. The Prachers got off in Alexandria, intending to rejoin the ship in Port Said. It was while the *Achille Lauro* was sailing between Alexandria and Port Said that a crew member, perhaps because of the suspicions raised, discovered the arms cache. The Palestinians panicked, pulled out weapons, and began firing their automatic weapons to scare off crew and passengers. They then quickly took charge of the bridge and of the radio room and captured the *Achille Lauro*.

The hijackers decided to have the ship leave Egyptian waters as quickly as possible and sailed for Syria. The Syrian navy would have none of it. That was what really panicked the terrorists and caused them to execute Leon Klinghoffer, the ritual killing designed to exert control and have people pay attention to their demands.

This caused a problem for the PLO. The *Achille Lauro* was to be used as a means of undetected transportation of a terrorist team into an Israeli port. Instead it turned into the hijacking of an Italian ship. Fortunately, Arafat still had the respect of the Palestinians as their leader, and he could see that the hijackers surrendered. In effect, Arafat was saying to his militants: Now is not the time.

On October 10, a spokesman for Mohammed Abul Abbas's faction of the Palestine Liberation Front delivered a statement to Reuters, apologizing to the passengers for the hijacking—perhaps the first time that any Arab terrorist group has expressed regret for an outrage. By panicking, the men who seized the *Achille Lauro* managed to elicit condemnation not only in the West but from the Arab world as well. But this mismanaged terrorist act failed also in communications with headquarters. Two days after Klinghoffer was killed, the Mohammed Abul Abbas group's "apology" released in Nicosia said, "It is important to us to emphasize that there is no truth whatsoever to reports that one of the passengers was killed. These reports are designed by the Zionist enemy to exploit the circumstances surrounding the operation in order to cover up its own crimes against the Palestinian people."

Passengers and crew put the lie to the Palestinian statement. And Leon Klinghoffer's body, bearing two bullet wounds when it washed ashore, confirmed it.

In some ways the ending to the *Achille Lauro* affair— one hesitates to call such a terrifying experience a fiasco, but from the terrorists' point of view that's what it turned out to be—had several benefits for the war against terrorism.

First, it demonstrated how anxious Egypt, Italy, and Yugoslavia were to appease the terrorists. Egypt's first instinct was to lie in order to let all the terrorists get away. Italy and Yugoslavia, to their everlasting shame, let the leader, Mohammed Abul Abbas, and his military chief, Kan, get away. And it is the leaders who should be the prime target in the antiterrorist war. The actions of Egypt, Italy, and Yugoslavia helped once more to give appeasement the bad name it deserves.

The second benefit of this farcical hijacking was the finesse with which the American military reaction resulted in the waylaying of Egyptair 737. It was applauded with some reservations around the world.

Very quickly after a terrorist incident, as, sadly, the Americans have demonstrated, resolve seems to evaporate. Within three months of the *Achille Lauro* incident, the Rome and Vienna airports were attacked on December 27, 1985, and American citizens killed and wounded. The United States responded slowly, thoughtfully, and inadequately. It should have ordered all U.S. citizens out of Libya within twenty-four hours instead of thirty days. Yes, it would have been very inconvenient for those people, but the purpose of such an action would have been to prevent them from being taken hostage and would have declared a decisive policy. It might also have had an effect in making Great Britain and France feel more vulnerable in caring for their greater number of potential hostages in Libya. Immediate reaction would most of all have tested the Libyan leader Qaddafi's priorities and increased his dread of retaliation. It was another real chance for the West to cause Qaddafi to face the consequences of his actions. Instead, the West mumbled and humbled itself and spoke in dissident voices, with the loudest of all, the United States, reassuring Qaddafi that no strike would take place now. He was let off the hook when precisely the opposite should have been done.

Of course, in the meantime the United States spent three months preparing three aircraft carrier battleship groups (again an armada) to challenge Qaddafi's "line of death" across the top of the Gulf of Sidra. One has to confront the fundamental question: does the sinking of attack gunboats or the blasting of antiaircraft facilities have any *lasting* effect on the war against the terrorists?

The intercept of the Egyptian plane carrying the *Achille Lauro* hijackers to safety was a direct action against terrorists and their leaders. It demonstrated the will and the ability for "hot pursuit" and capture. It had to give the planners of future terrorist attacks pause. Perhaps next time the leaders like Mohammed Abul Abbas and Kan would not be allowed to get away safely.

As *The New York Times* said, "One intercept does not an antiterrorism policy make."

As I have said previously, in fashioning an effective antiterrorism policy, the first step is to recognize that the terrorists are at war with the world. The second step is to recognize that appeasing terrorists is counterproductive. It doesn't work. The third step is to assess the value of retaliation, which we will now do.

11

Retaliation

There is something childish or adolescent in the idea of "getting even." That's what kids do, and kid gangs do especially. In the international arena, the morality of *West Side Story* has far greater consequences. We can perhaps best understand why retaliation doesn't work by tracing its unhappy history in recent times in the conflict between the Israelis and the Palestinians.

From the mid 1930s to 1948, terrorism was employed by extremists on both sides. Jew and Arab committed atrocities against each other and against the British occupiers of Palestine.

Israel's formal army, called the Haganah, bred officers with vision, such as Moshe Dayan, who as a young guide on oil pipeline patrols had come under the influence of a British officer named Charles Orde Wingate, later of Chindits fame in the second world war. I hold Dayan and Wingate in the highest regard as both soldiers and leaders of men.

But Israel also had two extremist groups, the Irgun Zvai Leumi, and Lechi, which was better known as the Stern Gang. After Israel was declared an independent state in

May of 1948, David Ben Gurion, leader of the Haganah and first Prime Minister of Israel, had the brilliance to deal with the extremists forcefully. On September 20, 1948, Haganah's Chief of Staff, Yigal Yadin, issued an ultimatum to both Jewish extremist groups: disband and hand over your arms and join the Haganah within twenty-four hours or suffer the full wrath of the army. What Ben Gurion did was to harness the aggression of the two extremist groups and offer them an alternative. It had the desired effect. The men and the skills were integrated into the army and into the Israeli intelligence services, later called Shin Beth and Mossad.

The extremists among the Arab Palestinians were not absorbed before they had "nowhere to go." Along with 600,000 displaced Palestinians, extremism traveled like a symbolic sword. But there was no nationalist leadership or cohesive strength among the Arabs, who spent their energies hating the Israelis and fighting each other, too.

You are going to be watching a scenario for a disaster that really happened, a Ping-Pong game that took many hundreds of lives and had absolutely no effect on the terrorist war. It was as futile as Vietnam was for the Americans, and for its allies, I might add, whose blood, including my own, stained that ground, too.

In response to every major terrorist outrage there are influential people who call for retaliation.

Retaliation, in simpler language, means tit for tat, an eye for an eye.

Tit for tat may momentarily quench the thirst for vengeance. It may make a politician feel that he is doing something. It may make the public feel that the politicians are doing something. But tit for tat *sends no message to the enemy*. It is merely an invitation for him to think up some bigger or better response. If tit for tat balloons, it can become a costly and useless conventional war as it did when Israel invaded Lebanon.

Let's zero in on Jerusalem, June 22, 1968. An Arab bomb

explodes in the marketplace. Toll: fourteen dead, a very cost effective exploit for the terrorists.

During the next twelve months the Palestinians, operating out of nearby Jordan and Egypt, carried out intense terrorist activity against Israel. Rocket and shellfire was directed from Jordan onto Eilat and other villages along the border, shelling civilians. Bombs went off in Haifa as well as Jerusalem. There were attacks on El Al aircraft in Zurich and Athens. Another El Al plane was hijacked to Algeria.

The Israelis, of course, responded with regularity. The Israeli military, still riding high on their astonishing quick victory in the Six-Day War, reacted to terrorist activity with helicopter-borne commandos going after targets in Jordan and Egypt. They destroyed electrical installations, bridges, dams such as the Nag Gammadi near Luxor, and the Ghor Canal in Jordan.

The message the Israelis were trying to send to the Egyptian and Jordanian governments was: If you offer safe haven to Palestinian terrorists, that is an act of war against Israel, and Israel will strike back. Jordan began to listen. Egypt turned a deaf ear.

Lebanon was also providing safe havens for Palestinians. To get a message across, on December 28, 1968, the Israelis raided the Beirut airport and destroyed thirteen civilian aircraft on the ground. The Palestinians couldn't care less about the civilian planes. They received no message. And the Lebanese couldn't control them even if they wanted to.

Then the Israelis struck at the Egyptian military headquarters at Manqubad and killed more than a hundred Egyptians in a daring raid. Did the Palestinian terrorists care? The Egyptians, forever concerned with saving face, could only encourage the terrorists to exact revenge.

Israel's policy of retaliation had no effect in stopping terrorist activity. The Palestinians struck at Israel abroad and at home.

On August 29, 1969, the PFLP hijacked TWA Flight 840, a 707 enroute from Rome to Tel Aviv, and had it put down in Damascus, Syria. On the ground, the hijackers blew up the cockpit. Several passengers were injured evacuating the plane. The Syrians released all the passengers except six Israelis. These were exchanged many months later, on December 5, for thirteen Syrians and fifty-eight Egyptians held in Israel.

Meanwhile, on September 2, 1969, Palestinians, using a Soviet-made rocket system, fired Katyusha shells at the towns of Qiryat Shemona and Kfar Giladi, killing three and wounding seven.

The Israeli government took retaliatory action that month. They used their air force and heliborne troops in attacks across their borders, this time more precisely targeting the Palestinian enclaves out of which the PFLP was operating.

By narrowing their focus, the Israelis hoped that the terrorists themselves and not just their hosts would get the message. But retaliation of such grand scale sends no message, it is merely a stimulus for further provocation. The big hammer is seen to indiscriminately crush wives, children, etc., and hatred is further fueled.

And so the Palestinians *escalated* their attacks, broadening them to include Europe and Europeans, sending a message that it is dangerous to be involved with the Israelis, even as passengers on their airliners. Early in 1970, a bus carrying El Al passengers at Munich airport was attacked by Palestinians with hand grenades. One El Al passenger was killed, eleven wounded.

The next message was targeted at the Swiss, who, though neutral in conventional warfare, were holding three PFLP terrorists who had shot up an El Al plane in Zurich and killed the copilot. Black September wanted their release, and so eleven days after the bus episode at Munich the Palestinians destroyed a Swiss airliner in midflight, killing forty-seven people, and accomplishing absolutely nothing for the Palestinian cause, except to get more people involved.

What Israel did with both of these messages was to move faster in making El Al one of the safest airlines in the world to travel on. Unfortunately, that was not a lot of use to the rest of the world's travelers. The Israelis also decided that since the terrorists were broadening their targets, perhaps the Israelis should narrow theirs. On March 5, 1970, they sent a small commando force across the Dead Sea into Jordan and attacked a Palestinian safe house, killing three and taking three terrorists captive for interrogation. As a result of the information gained from harsh interrogation, the Israelis launched commando raids at specific targets in Lebanon and air strikes on identified Palestinian terrorist camps in Syria.

These targeted attacks were not seen as prevention but as further retaliation. Israeli action was headed in the right direction, but the message wasn't clear. On May 20, 1970, Arab terrorists did what they do best. They attacked a bus carrying children with a bazooka. They killed twelve and wounded nineteen. Then they geared up for a really big show, a spectacular that would concentrate the world's attention on their fight for their lost Palestine.

On September 6, 1970, in a coordinated effort, the Palestinians hijacked five airliners.

Only one of the five was an El Al airliner. The sky marshals aboard were trained Israeli counterterrorists who were able to thwart the hijacking. Successfully hijacked were a TWA 707 flying from Frankfurt to New York, and an Air India VC10 scheduled to go from London to India via Bahrain. All three, in a well-coordinated plan, ended up at a deserted airstrip in Jordan called Dawson's Field. The fifth plane, a Pan Am 707, departing Amsterdam for New York, was forced to fly to Cairo. There the passengers and crew escaped down evacuation chutes before the plane was blown up with prelaid explosives.

With three large aircraft on the ground at Dawson, the

PFLP let the world know its demands. They wanted the release of terrorist superstar Leila Khaled, the three PFLP members held in West Germany for the attack on the airline bus in Munich, plus the three held in Switzerland. They also demanded the release of an unspecified number of fedayeen held in Israel. Captured terrorists in prison, then as now, are an invitation to further terrorist acts.

The negotiations between the hijackers and the nations holding the prisoners were protracted and led nowhere. The hijackers, their planes covered by cameras, decided to benefit at least from a media event and blew up the planes at Dawson. The forty remaining hostages were carried off and imprisoned in Palestinian refugee camps in Amman.

King Hussein of Jordan, an educated, civilized head of state genuinely interested in Middle East peace, had had enough. He used the Jordanian army to rescue the hostages. In bitter fighting, his British-trained troops were able to remove the Palestinian terrorist presence from his kingdom.

The Palestinians then went through a period of reorganization, with the Black September offshoot of the PFLP coming to the fore. Also, terrorist factions were relocated with two serious consequences: Lebanon, to Israel's north, became the principal terrorist base, and the PFLP forged strong links with European terrorist groups so that the war of retaliation could continue.

IT IS IMPORTANT to note here what kind of targets the terrorists prefer, else we shall never understand the difference between terrorists and revolutionaries. On July 7, 1971, when the Palestinians had gotten their act back together again, they launched a rocket attack on a hospital and a school near the town of Petah Tikva in Israel, killing four and wounding sixteen. In wars prior to the present, hospitals, with their clearly marked Red or Blue Crosses, were usually exempt from specific attack. And schoolchildren became targets only in massive bombing raids on whole cities. But the terrorist mind seeks out the previously exempt. Hospitals and schools became *preferred* targets. The world, which reacted with universal abhorrence to the events at My Lai in Vietnam, needs to understand that actions perceived as atrocities are exactly what the terrorists have in mind.

The Israeli response was large. Four hundred Israeli paratroopers raided Palestinian bases at Yater and Kifr in Lebanon with anger and poor results: twelve dead and five wounded.

The terrorist target net then spread to encompass their new enemy: Jordan. On February 6, 1972, Black September terrorists, by now recognized as the bloodthirstiest of the Palestinian splinter groups, assassinated five Jordanian workers in Cologne, Germany, labeling their fellow Arabs as "spies for Israel." These five were fingered by a Jordanian Palestinian.

On May 8, 1972, four members of Black September hijacked a Belgian Sabena airliner flying the Vienna/Athens/Tel Aviv route, and forced it to land at Lod Airport in Tel Aviv. That was a mistake. The hijackers demanded the release of 317 Palestinians imprisoned in Israel. What they got was a cleverly contrived commando exercise by Israeli paratroopers. First, they deflated the tires of the aircraft so it couldn't go anywhere. Then, commandos dressed as ground service personnel suddenly stormed the aircraft, killing both male hijackers and wounding one of the women. It wasn't a perfect raid, for five passengers were wounded, one of whom subsequently died. But it showed determination not to give in to the demands of the hijackers. The two female hijackers received long sentences.

Terrorist leaders brooded over this defeat. They decided to use their linkage to perpetrate an outrage that the Israelis would be unable to cope with. Before the end of the month, on May 30, 1972, three Japanese Red Army members on loan to the Palestinians, playing in their minds the traditional mercenary role of the Samurai warrior, smiling and polite, opened their bags at Lod Airport and, using machine guns and hand grenades, killed twenty-six bystanders and wounded seventy-six. One of the Japanese terrorists, Kozo Okomoto, mentioned earlier, was captured alive. This was to prove significant. The Israelis are proficient in getting a prisoner to talk.

On September 5, 1972, in full view of a watching world, Black September terrorists struck at the Olympic Village in Munich, killed several Israeli athletes, and held those who did not escape hostage. This was to have several profound effects, one leading to effective retaliation by a Mossad hit team seeking out and killing a number of leading Arab terrorists throughout Europe until their vengeance got the better of them, leading to a mistaken killing.

At the time of the Munich massacre, Abu Nidal was in the leadership of Black September, but the actual organizer of the massacre was Abu Iyad. The weapons were supplied by Fakhri al-Umari. Another Black September leader, Abu Daoud, was on the massacre assault team, using the alias of Saad ad-din Wali. Other team members included Yusuf Nazzal and Mohammed Masalhah. The latter was highly qualified to carry out his role of reconnaissance. Masalhah was one of the architects who had worked on the construction of the Olympic Village! All told, there were eight terrorists in the assault.

No one familiar with the event will forget how the terrorists and their surviving hostages were airlifted by helicopter to Furstenfeldbruck airfield, a military base outside Munich, where the demanded plane was ostensibly being readied for their escape. There the German police, then ill-trained in work of this sort, attempted an ill-fated ambush to kill the terrorists. This horribly mismanaged affair resulted in all the hostages being killed, left five of the terrorists dead, and resulted in the death of one of the policemen. Munich Chief of Police Schreiber later commented, "Some people say that it was police mistakes that caused the death of the hostages, but it was the other way around. The death of the hostages was caused because the terrorists made no mistakes."

The Israelis, of course, were stunned. The Germans were equally stunned. Out of this mortifying event, one good thing happened: GSG9 was born, the special unit trained to SAS standards in counterterrorism, and now one of the best such professional forces in the world.

The three of the eight Munich terrorists who were arrested rather than killed did not have a long wait in prison. Seven weeks later, on October 29, 1972, Lufthansa flight 615 from Damascus to Frankfurt was hijacked by two soldiers of Black September. They found the Germans in a placating mood. The plane and its passengers were bartered for the three surviving Munich terrorists, who were turned over to the Yugoslavs. From Zagreb, they flew to Libya and, undoubtedly, high honors for one of the most successful terrorist outrages in memory. Had GSG9 been operative at the time of Munich, there likely would have been no terrorist survivors.

The Israelis, angered beyond belief at the Munich Massacre, retaliated in force. They launched a series of air attacks on Palestinian bases in Lebanon and Syria, particularly along the Beirut-Damascus highway. This was the opposite of a counterterrorist action. It was a major assault employing jets, tanks, and 3,000 troops. The result was miniscule in relation to the effort. Approximately fifty Arabs were killed, some of them undoubtedly terrorists, and about a hundred houses were destroyed. I have said before that terrorist actions are cost-effective (witness the Munich massacre). Retaliation by massive conventional military means is not. It means escalation and, to the terrorists' delight, the involvement of global politics.

DURING THE PERIOD September/October 1972, the Palestinians and the Israelis started exchanging mail. On September 9, 1972, the Israeli Consul in London was killed by a letter bomb. The London Metropolitan Police took swift action to try to stop further such killings on British soil. They made no secret that they would have preferred that all the targets uncovered by intelligence just leave Britain and receive their letter bombs elsewhere. All in all, the British police intercepted more than forty letter bombs, all posted in Amsterdam. A second batch of letter bombs, these mailed from Malaysia, were also successfully intercepted. The counterterrorist intelligence network and increased cooperation between countries since Munich was paying off.

In the dance of retaliation, the Israelis responded to this deadly adolescent charade by posting letter bombs in Belgrade addressed to Palestinian leaders in Lebanon, Libya, Egypt, and Algeria. In desperation, they resorted to the technique of the terrorist, as they had against the British in the 1940s.

In addition to the major military action that had minimal results, the Israeli response to Munich was the organization of the now-famous hit team that was turned loose in Europe to get the terrorists responsible.

Wael Zwaiter had the cover job of clerk at the Libyan Embassy in Rome. Actually, he was the local representative of Al Fatah. The Mossad had identified him as the organizer of the Lod massacre, probably through their intensive interrogation of the surviving Japanese Red Army member, Okomoto. Zwaiter publicly claimed that the Israelis themselves had carried out the Munich massacre. That signed his death sentence. On December 8, 1972, he was killed outside his apartment by the Mossad's revenge squad.

On the same day that they got Wael Zwater for putting the blame of Munich on the Israelis, other members of the team went after Mahmoud Hamshari in Paris. Hamshari's primary role in France had been recruiting French militants for Black September operations, using the cover of a theatrical group playing at a west Paris theater called the Téâtre de l'Ouest. Though his role in connection with Munich was unclear, his link to Black September was not, and for the Israeli hit team that was enough. On December 8, 1972, he was killed by a bomb attached to his telephone.

But eventually, and perhaps inevitably, the hit squad hit the wrong person. In a classic case of mistaken identity, a Moroccan waiter was gunned down in front of his pregnant wife in Norway. This scandalous mistargeting is what results from obsession with revenge and retaliation. The month-long vendetta ended in tragedy. The result was an outcry against Israeli methods. There were furious exchanges in the Israeli Knesset (Parliament) about the morality of revenge. One could say that if the only good terrorist is a dead terrorist, the Israeli hit squad did well. But the waiter was not a terrorist.

Not unexpectedly then, while Israel searched its soul, Black September gunned down an Israeli intelligence officer in a Madrid cafe on January 26, 1973, claiming he was involved in the killing of Hamshari and Zwaiter (killed in Paris and Rome respectively on the same day).

When seen in tandem, these retaliatory exchanges appear futile.

The next move was the Israelis'. On April 10, Israeli Commandos raided the Beirut headquarters of the PFLP and Black September. This targeted attack made more sense from a prevention point of view. The Israelis killed fifteen Palestinian terrorists on this raid but also picked up some intelligence data that enabled them to track down at least one Arab terrorist operating in Europe, Mohammed Boudia. Boudia was an important organizer of terrorist outrages, including raids in Rotterdam and on West German factories. In Paris, the Mossad placed a bomb under the driver's seat of Boudia's car. When he turned the ignition on, he was blown to bits.

Though the Israelis, in targeting Palestinian terrorists, could be seen moving from retaliation to prevention, the

PLO and its offshoots decided to bring the Mideast terrorist tit for tat to U.S. soil. No one could remember the last time when a foreign diplomat accredited to Washington had been killed. And no Israeli official had ever been hit in the United States. Then the Palestinians struck.

Colonel Yosef Alon, a well-known Israeli fighter pilot ace, was Deputy Military Attache of the Israeli Embassy in Washington. He, his wife, and three daughters aged 5, 14, and 18 lived in a ranch-style house in Chevy Chase, Maryland, a Washington suburb. Colonel Alon and his wife Deborah were returning from a farewell party for one of his embassy colleagues at about 1:00 A.M. on July 1, 1973. Deborah Alon got out of the car first and was on the porch when she heard five shots near their car parked in the driveway. She let herself into the house and quickly phoned for help. When she came out she found her husband had been shot in the chest five times and was dying. Neighbors later told the police they'd heard the shots and a car speeding away.

U.S. authorities tried to pass the killing off as an attempted robbery though President Nixon immediately ordered the Secret Service to step up protection of diplomats in Washington. Even the Israeli Embassy fudged, saying "We're careful not to jump to any conclusions." But the Voice of Palestine, broadcasting in Arabic from Cairo, crowed that Colonel Alon had been executed in retaliation for the death of Mohammed Boudia in Paris three days earlier. A State Department official said one couldn't tell from the broadcast whether the Palestinians were claiming responsibility for the killing or were merely seizing it as an opportunity for propaganda. Five shots in the chest and a car speeding away in seconds didn't sound like a robbery to any of us in the counterterrorist community. This hit underscored how vulnerable the previously untouched Washington, D.C., area had become to a very fast retaliation for an execution in Europe.

A MONTH LATER, on August 5, 1973, a TWA plane out of Tel
Aviv landed at Athens and was attacked by young terrorists. As it so often has, Athens appears again in the catalog
of terrorist drama. The terrorists managed sixty casualties, five dead, fifty-five wounded. Two of the Arabs were
captured, sentenced to death—and released, of course, in
response to demands of hijackers the following February.

On December 17, 1973, five Palestinian terrorists opened
fire in the customs area of the Leonardo da Vinci Airport in
Rome, Italy. The terrorists took several hostages, pro-
ceeded to a Pan-Am 707 that was loading for a flight to
Beirut, and threw three hand grenades into the plane,
killing or injuring numerous passengers. The terrorists
with their hostages than boarded and hijacked a Lufthansa aircraft to Athens and Kuwait, where the hijackers
surrendered. Significantly, the hijackers were flown to
Cairo on March 2, 1974, where they were to be tried by the
PLO, but the Egyptian authorities would not release them.
They were eventually released in November 1974 on the
demand of the other *fedayeen* hijackers and went on to
Libya.

On the last day of the year, Lord Sieff, president of the
giant Marks and Spencer department store chain and a
British Jew who strongly supported Israel, was shot in the
face in his London home, supposedly by Carlos, who was
then in charge of linking up the Western European terrorist groups with the Arabs. Lord Sieff made a miraculous
recovery, the bullet having ricocheted off his teeth.

In 1974 there was intensive terrorist activity against
Israel. On April 11, eight members of a Palestinian assault
team, part of a group calling itself "Jibril's Front," entered
Israel proper through Lebanon and killed eighteen people
at Qiryat.

One could feel Israeli frustration ticking like a time
bomb. Israel made a number of raids into Lebanon with
the main aim of destroying houses involved in the Palestinian attacks.

As the Israelis concentrated their attention on specific

terrorist targets, the Palestinians continued to select non-military targets and to perpetrate assaults that, instead of aiding the Palestinian cause, threatened to alienate the civilized world from them.

On May 15, 1974, three Palestinian terrorists occupied a school at Ma'alot. The attempt to relieve the hostage situation was badly handled. The terrorists killed twenty-five and wounded sixty-two, including many children.

Then on June 13, 1974, Arab terrorist commandos crossed from Lebanon into Israel to carry out an attack that would signify a change to a more deadly approach. They killed three people in a *kibbutz,* but the attackers were not carrying sufficient weaponry to defend themselves and had no possible lines of retreat, which meant that they didn't intend to hit and run. It was a suicide mission, the beginning of a new phase.

On October 8, 1974, again Greece, again TWA. A flight that originated in Israel, stopped in Athens, and then, having left Athens, was blown up in mid-air with all eighty-eight people aboard killed.

Meanwhile, the terrorist acts inside Israel continued. In Beit Shean, an Arab terrorist assault team managed to effect more than 200 casualties. On December 11, a bomb exploded in a Tel Aviv theater, with sixty-five casualties. Less than three months later an eight-man Fatah suicide squad occupied the Savoy Hotel in Tel Aviv, killed eleven, and wounded the same number before they themselves fell.

The multinational training of linked terrorist groups—including Europeans in Palestinian camps—increased at a frightening level. Finally, on June 27, 1976, a joint commando band of the German Baader-Meinhof gang and PFLP terrorists began an exercise that had a marked effect on the world's view of counterterrorist activity. The German-Arab terrorists hijacked an Air France Airbus with some Jewish passengers to Entebbe in Uganda, where the madman's army of Idi Amin would protect the terrorists.

The Entebbe raid by Israeli commandos was led by

someone I knew and admired, Yani Netanyahu. The raid was to specialists in the field an exemplary exercise in logistics, planning, and execution, but relatively easy to accomplish once the commandos got to Entebbe because the Ugandan soldiers, on a scale of zero to ten, would show up below the line. However, there were the multinational terrorists to deal with, and seven of them were killed on the spot and all but one of the hostages rescued unscathed. That one passenger, a Mrs. Bloch, a bone stuck in her throat, had been removed to a hospital in Entebbe. After the successful raid, the miserably humiliated Ugandan troops dragged the elderly woman from her hospital bed and slaughtered her.

There was one other casualty. The leader of the commandos, Netanyahu, was shot and killed by one of the Ugandans. It was a high price to pay, but the Israelis reestablished the arm with the long reach. It seems significant that, as of this writing, a decade has gone by since Entebbe and no Israeli aircraft has been hijacked because of the special preventive measures they take.

THE ASSAULTS ON Israel now increasingly took the form of random rocket attacks from Lebanon on civilian farming settlements. Finally, the response escalated. This time, in March 1978, the Israelis, reluctant to return to the unpalatable assassination techniques of post-Munich, committed 20,000 troops, supported by artillery and air cover, to the occupation of a ten-mile-wide area inside the Lebanese frontier. The intent was to stop the rocket attacks. The result was disastrous for Israeli domestic politics and, for the first time, challenged world opinion normally in sympathy with Israel. It was being sucked into a war with increasing speed. The Israelis' frustration and traditionally single-minded approach blinded them to the predictable consequences of their strategy.

On March 11, 1978, a nine-man PLO squad audaciously landed on a beach north of Tel Aviv. They took 46 hos-

tages. The Israelis counterattacked. In the ensuing gun-
fight, all forty-six hostages and all nine terrorists were
killed, and more than 170 Israelis were wounded.

Thereafter the PLO took to bombs again. They put one in
a children's toy store in Tel Aviv, wounding fifty people. A
bomb placed in a bus en route to Jerusalem killed four and
wounded thirty-seven.

On August 20, 1978, Palestinian terrorists in London
attacked an El Al crew bus outside a hotel, killing one and
wounding one.

Inside Israel, Ma'alot was again attacked. This time a
rest home was the target.

The Israelis' response went increasingly to Lebanon. A
captured terrorist, under strong interrogation (a euphem-
ism), revealed the exact location of Ali Hassan Salameh, a
terrorist long hunted unsuccessfully by an Israeli hit team.
He was in Beirut. On January 22, 1979, the Israeli military
attacked in a carefully planned operation. They killed
Salameh and four others. The Israeli war machine began
to roll, and air strikes and naval bombardments aimed at
Palestinian camps and villages in the south of Lebanon
increased.

The final escalation of the retaliatory response was the
Israeli invasion of Lebanon on June 6, 1982, and the beginning of a war that would involve the world's active
participation through the intervention of a United Nations
peacekeeping force. The extreme Arab factions rejoiced at
this widening involvement: the foreign policies of major
nations were exposed in disarray and American, British,
and French peacekeeping troops became sitting ducks in
the ensuing carnage.

The real victims, of course, were the Lebanese people and
their identity as a nation. I recall Beirut and the country at
large as a place of beauty, civility, and vitality. My last
visits during 1983 and 1984 were operational, and I found
myself in a country ravaged by war. Beirut was unrecog-
nizable as a city, and the people were desperately trying to

go about life amidst the chaos. I observed all this misery and destruction and remember thinking: All this because the politicians couldn't work it out with any vision in Palestine way back in 1948.

The irony is that the terrorist world became stronger and more cohesive. The historic Islamic brotherhood, which spawned El Fatah and the PFLP, Black September, and the other offshoots, had gained enormous momentum from what had amounted to the humiliation of the United States and, in the Arab view, its puppet Israel. If we think a problem started with the partition of Palestine, the events of 1984 in Lebanon had better concentrate our minds.

The facts are obvious. Unless retaliation is designed to prevent escalation, the results are catastrophic. Israeli retaliation was most effective when the policy was to hunt down and kill known terrorist leaders. One mistake in a deadly war, the killing in Norway of the Moroccan, Ahmed Bouchki, and the timid response and subsequent soul-searching that followed, cost the Israelis and others dearly. It led to the Knesset stopping the practice of seeking out and executing terrorists wherever they might be found.

Terrorism can be likened to a well-prepared ambush. The choices we are presented with are: to keep walking into that ambush and continue to take heavy casualties; not to venture out, avoid the ambush, and in effect capitulate to terror; or to take the war to the terrorist and in so doing contain the fight and prevent the ambush. It seems that the only sensible choice must be prevention.

12

Prevention

There is a conflict between the religious teachings that have had a major influence on the way society moralizes. The Bible and the Koran invoke "an eye for an eye," a policy I have just described as retaliation. The Hebrew Talmud says, "If someone comes to kill you, rise and kill him first." That is prevention. In less theological terms, teachings of military history have for centuries advocated attack as the best means of defense.

It is a old saw that an ounce of prevention is worth a pound of cure. When it comes to stopping terrorism, prevention is a multipurpose response: it saves the lives of future victims, it saves the huge cost of armadas and air strikes for rescue or retaliation, and it avoids the cul-de-sac of escalation that governments invariably find themselves driven into.

When it comes to moving against terrorism, the responses of the Western democracies could be characterized as "either too little and most often too late." The intelligence information available from a variety of sources on the terrorists is now superb. Law enforcement, however, is often unwilling or unable to use the knowledge gained.

Take the case of Zuhair Akkasha, who was well known
not only in counterterrorist circles but to the London police
as a Palestinian fanatic capable of murderous action. On
December 15, 1975, Akkasha appeared in a London courtroom, charged with assaulting a policeman. This was no
subtle plotter or devious Carlos, moving along a well-
prepared underground network of safe houses and sympathizers and going to most elaborate lengths to avoid being
noticed. And a clever terrorist would try not to be noticed.
Not so Akkasha. He was noticed, but the British police
failed to spot his real potential.

For his assault against a police officer, Akkasha was
sentenced to six months in jail and deportation. He served
his (short) time and was expelled. Within a year he was
back. An observant policeman spotted him in Wimpy bar.
He was followed and seen going into a building in a row of
inexpensive accommodations. The observation was duti-
fully relayed to Scotland Yard, but unfortunately the significance of the sighting went unheeded.

Two months later, Akkasha waited impatiently in the
lobby of the Royal Lancaster Hotel. At last he spotted his
quarry in the back seat of a car in front of the hotel.
Akkasha opened the back door and shot to death former
Yemeni Prime Minister Cadi Abdullah al-Hajari, his wife
Fatima, and embassy diplomat Abdullah al-Hammani.

Whoever in Scotland Yard was tipped off about Akkasha's return to London and decided to do nothing about
it was negligent and not awake to the war on his doorstep.
Three people paid with their lives. A further death was to
result.

Although the triple murder was committed in public on a
street in central London, Akkasha got away. Six months
later he surfaced again as one of those responsible for the
hijacking of a Lufthansa plane and forcing it to land at
Mogadishu. Akkasha, the man Scotland Yard neglected,
was identified as the hijacker who shot the pilot, Jurgen
Schumann. When the GSG9 team successfully assaulted

the hijacked aircraft, Akkasha was one of the terrorists killed, a just end to his career.

There are at least two lessons to be learned from the Akkasha case. Terrorists tend to escalate their outrages. And if you let a terrorist get away, he'll come back to haunt you. If he commits his next outrage against an ally, that ally won't be grateful.

Deporting a known terrorist does not mean a country is successfully exporting his trouble-making capacity. It is setting him free and washing its hands of the problem. The terrorist skips off to a country that presumably welcomes his return. After an interval, that same terrorist could come right back into the country that deported him and commit further atrocities. Terrorism is not a national but an international problem. According to the U.S. State Department, both the French and Italian governments have had secret pacts that permitted terrorists to pass in and out of their countries with impunity as long as they committed terrorist acts elsewhere! The shortsightedness of such policies is self-evident, as both France and Italy learned in the arcade and airport attacks committed in December 1985 in Paris and Rome.

A policy of prevention requires that living, active terrorists be detained, not released; if deported, they should be sent only to a country that wants to try them for crimes committed there and not to countries that offer terrorists safe havens and rest periods until their next offense; and allies should act like allies and not permit known terrorists of any nationality to plot, plan, and move about with impunity on the assumption that their outrages will be committed elsewhere in the free world.

MOST OF TODAY'S terrorism has been born out of past political expediency. That expediency produces betrayal and distrust, even among supposed allies. I have witnessed its bloody results in many countries.

If we acknowledge that the terrorists are at war with us, I

must ask in what other kind of war could the enemy be allowed to walk around in your city streets in complete safety? Until we send—and terrorists everywhere get—the message that they are not safe *anywhere* in the Western democracies, we will continue losing the terrorist war.

THE HARD SIDE of prevention is upsetting to a lot of people, so let us deal with the soft side first.

The American and French embassies in Beirut were the objects of successful car bombings. The truck bombing of the Marine barracks that left 241 dead was the last straw. It should have inspired the introduction of a layered defense system at all military establishments, embassies, and nuclear facilities. By layered defense, I mean pushing the defensive perimeter away from the hub of the facility so that the first security obstacle a terrorist would have to confront is at a sufficient distance from the target to allow intermediate layers to close up and render the threat harmless.

A layered defense is the first ounce of prevention. The second is the kind of training and mind-set that is needed by embassy guards in a terrorist atmosphere. Embassy guards can no longer afford to be just a ceremonial force, chosen for the men's precision drilling. They must be of a caliber that can be trusted to shoot to kill a selected oncoming target, even if approaching through a crowd of innocent passers-by. They must also remain disciplined and alert, regardless of the tedium that accompanies all guard duty.

If any facility allows for an extended approach by vehicle, disguised reinforced obstacles should be installed to defeat the possibility of a vehicle accelerating with the intent to mount steps or force an entry, such as the truck bomber successfully did. These obstacles, which are in effect tank traps, will obviously be camouflaged in such a way as to blend with the normally peaceful environment. A well thought out example are the oversized flowerpots that have appeared, strategically placed in front of the American Embassy in London. Not only do they display beautiful flowers, but I daresay that the engineers who sunk the prestressed steel through them, and deep into the ground beneath, insured that each flowerpot was strong enough to stop a tank.

A well-protected facility with extended approaches must have—and be known to both guards and visitors as having—a predetermined killing ground. Once the alarm is given, there must be an area that is a point of no return. On visiting the guardhouse at the perimeter, visitors will be fully briefed on the existence of this killing ground and what to do if they happen to be caught in it when an alarm goes off. The normal order will be to halt or lie down on the spot, in the clear knowledge that anyone moving about in the killing area after the alarm has sounded is liable to be shot.

Where feasible, guard units assigned to the killing-ground area should be equipped with a shoulder-fired portable antiarmor weapon, with the firm order to use it if the terrorist vehicle and driver cannot be immobilized simultaneously by small arms fire. If the normal guards on duty are not up to such disciplined defense in this age of terrorism, the answer is simple. They must be replaced.

It is tragic that this kind of precaution should have to be taken in great centers of culture like London, Washington, Paris, and Rome. The blame must be laid at the door of politicians and statesmen whose foresight was less than 20/20. The Middle East issues that were left unresolved grew like mold in a petri dish. The Palestinians didn't fade away. Their anger simmered and was finally put to use in terrorist activities that spread over several continents and became, in the hands of fanatics, an end in itself and a danger to all the democracies. Did anyone imagine that the failures of diplomacy would result in the American Sixth Fleet, deployed at a cost of millions, crossing Qaddafi's "Line of Death" across the Gulf of Sidra, tempting

his Soviet-built missiles to fire, and then, when the skir-
mish was over, waiting for the inevitable: the cost-effective
response of terrorists blowing open a plane in mid-air,
sending three generations of an American family falling
through the sky to a horrible death; or a disco in West
Berlin exploding the lives of over 200 people, while the rest
of the so-called civilized world sat paralyzed in front of its
television sets, waiting to learn how next the terrorists
would administer their doses of death and fear.

In any democracy, nobody wants to live a fortress existence, or to be intimidated by a continual show of force such
as soldiers in the streets, or even to see the everyday cour-
tesies that exist within a free-moving society disappear.
Sadly, if ruthless preventive action toward terrorists is not
adopted, then the terrorist aim will have been achieved by
society's eventually immobilizing itself.

BUSINESSMEN ARE AWARE of their special vulnerability.
Chairmen of major corporations will have the resources to
obtain the best outside advice on security and to implement it. For those members of the general public and businessmen who feel threatened but who lack those resources,
the following thoughts and elementary suggestions may
be of help.

Businessmen travel a good deal. Of the 567 Americans
kidnapped abroad between 1970-78, more than half were
businessmen. Their facilities, depending on what business
they are in and where the plant is located, can be protected
just as government installations can. The specialized companies that advise large corporations on preventive measures can assess a particular company's vulnerability and
suggest solutions. They will show executives how they can
be provided with layers of protection with the least possible disruption of normal life. Their experience in such matters as staff screening, building security, driver training in
escape-and-evade techniques, body armor, and bullet-
resistant cars can all save valuable time.

But even an armored Mercedes or a bullet-resistant windshield that won't shatter if hit by a bullet will do no good if the executive's mind-set is careless. If the businessman's well-trained driver calls in sick but has gotten a "friend" to substitute, the executive would be wise to refuse the substitute and use another means of getting around while the driver's illness is investigated. Did he himself call in or did someone call in for him? Has the driver been kidnaped? Or paid off? In other words, the executive in a business or location that makes him vulnerable should develop a sense of preventive caution by being as suspicious as a counterterrorist must be even under everyday circumstances.

For the duration, because there is a war on.

Complacency is the businessman's worst enemy. Prevention is his best defense.

There are a number of tactics a businessman at risk should follow. (Diplomats and military officers attached to embassies in high risk areas should do the same.)

Never leave for work at the same time.

Give no clues that you are about to leave for work.

Do not leave by the same door. Do not follow a pattern in your use of alternate doors.

Have your car kept in a secure place overnight to prevent the attachment of a bomb.

Have your driver conspicuously start the car each morning and let the engine run for a while before you leave your house and enter your car. Also have the driver turn the wheels and move a few feet, then back up into place as he waits for you. (Car bombs can be linked to the ignition or to the turning of wheels.) A terrorist planning an attack doesn't want to kill only your driver. He wants to kill you or abduct you, and killing the driver is an ancillary act. If the terrorist casing your situation knows the driver is checking the car out, he may refrain from trying to use it as a means to destroy or capture you. If your driver or bodyguard won't follow these instructions, get another.

It is obvious that you shouldn't take the same route to work each day if you want to avoid an ambush. Some awfully dumb people take the same alternate route every other day. Or use the same route for the first or last part of the trip. All of that assists in an ambush. Be clever about variances in your route as if your life depended on it. It does.

The telephone in your home and office are dangerous instruments. Small devices can be placed in telephones that will explode when you answer. Who cleans your house and has access to your phones? Who cleans your office?

At this point the businessman and the diplomat may be ready to say: *Who wants to live like that?*

The answer: Someone who wants to stay alive.

A better answer: You don't have to live like that if your mind-set is ready for the preventive action that must be taken by the world now if we don't want to live in fear of terrorists.

BEFORE WE TOOK out the Basque terrorist leaders in the south of France, there was some nervousness about the creation of martyrs. That didn't happen. As I've pointed out, we not only got rid of a few "heroes" of ETA; their absence disrupted that terrorist group for years. But vigilance is needed to prevent new "heroes" from coming up.

One such potential hero had been a pillion passenger on the back of a Vespa motor scooter that drove up beside a Spanish Ministry of Defense car carrying an Army colonel to his office. The Vespa was sandwiched between the unprotected colonel's car and an innocent citizen driving himself to work. As the lights changed and the lines of traffic started to pull away toward the busy intersection of the picturesque Goya and its crowded sidewalks, the prospective ETA hero placed a satchel bomb on the roof of the colonel's car and accelerated away. Moments later, the car, the colonel, his driver, and the unsuspecting civilian driver on the other side of the sandwich were blown to oblivion.

The Vespa bomber became a newly promoted member of the terrorist operational committee. A party was organized to celebrate the promotion of the new hero. We had the party under nighttime surveillance. Three nights after the celebration, any ambitions the Vespa terrorist had of further heroic escapades were curtailed forever.

Prevention is clearly a continuing operation.

THE MONEY AND arms that are flowing to terrorists can both be interdicted if the will is there. I recall the time I was involved in a hurriedly conceived operation to dissuade a Greek shipowner and arms dealer, based in Athens, from transporting a large shipment of arms to the IRA.

A French colleague and I were dispatched by a certain department of a client government to explain to the wealthy Greek arms runner and his brother that we knew what they were up to and that their profitable but dirty business of supplying arms to terrorists had to stop at once.

Our instructions were that the shipment must be stopped and the source closed down. The first step was to get this emphatic message to the two Greeks.

The younger brother understood at once; he decided on short notice that their shipping office in Brindisi, Italy, required his immediate management. The older brother was a problem. He lived a life filled with opulent trappings, earned the same way drug barons make their millions—through trafficking in human misery. He simply dealt in weapons rather than drugs. His fortresslike home and his well-armed bodyguards made him both secure and arrogant. He thought the message my French colleague and I had brought was about money. He tried to buy us off with enormous bribes. He was still trying when, sitting in his car close to the airport in Athens, my French colleague delivered the message differently and shot him. He died, amazed to the very end that we had not come about money.

Cutting off the source of terrorist arms is second only to going after the terrorists themselves.

THE MIND-SET OF the Western democracies must come about like a yacht under sail when the wind changes. There has been a lot of talk about capturing terrorists and bringing them to trial, like Eichmann. How many show trials is the West ready for? Ten, thirty, a hundred? The terrorists will just keep coming. And what they will demand in exchange for the lives of new hostages is the release of their comrades and leaders being tried.

A detained terrorist is a danger.

A jailed terrorist will cause a new outrage.

We have to prepare our minds for the fact that when dealing with suicidal fanatics, the aim of counterterrorism is to kill terrorists and not to capture them. The only excuse for capturing a terrorist is to submit him to expert interrogation to obtain intelligence information about other terrorists or planned future terrorist acts.

Most people are not equipped to do this kind of work. (One wants to add "Thank God!") Civilians aren't. Law enforcement officials, police, are conditioned to capture, not kill. They also have legal prohibitions and strictures. The terrorists are a military force and must be dealt with by specially trained military personnel, as in the SAS, Delta, GSG9, and similar organizations, people used to working in small self-contained teams under the most adverse circumstances. At present, their work often has to be covert and deniable. The world is not yet ready to accept the idea that the terrorist war can be won by a policy of killing their leaders and all other active terrorists or terrorists-in-training who can be got at.

Almost all of them *can* be got at. It is the will that is still lacking.

Picture this. Enemy soldiers who have sworn to have a go at you whenever and wherever they can get at you are in a trench one hundred yards from your trench with a no man's land in between. You are holding your fire. Suddenly one of the enemy soldiers opens up and hits one of your men who had made the mistake of lifting his head a bit too high over the edge of the trench. Your man is dead. Do you order the others to fire *only on the one enemy soldier who opened fire* or on all of them?

I say it is wrong-headed, as some statesmen think, to fire only on the one enemy soldier who killed one of your people. All the men in the opposing trench would kill any or all of you if they had the opportunity. Don't waste a minute wondering if you are one of the targets. The terrorists know that the whole rest of the human race is their target. And if you are determined to fight back, *all* terrorists and terrorists-in-training are the people you go after. Otherwise you will be fighting the terrorist war till kingdom come. And if your first targets are the terrorist leaders, you'll win the war even more efficiently with fewer losses on your side.

I have never advocated any of the massive tactics that end up killing innocents. That's the terrorists's game, not mine.

In early 1986, a U.S. House of Representatives Judiciary Committee subcommittee approved a piece of legislation sponsored by Representative George W. Gekas of Pennsylvania that is well-intentioned and clearly wrong-headed. Representative Gekas's bill calls for the death penalty in terrorist incidents *in which Americans are killed.* I have risked my neck numerous times in hazardous operations for Americans. Does that mean that if I, a New Zealander, traveling aboard an American carrier, am killed in a terrorist incident, Representative Gekas would chalk that up to bad luck? What happened to "no man is an island?" Are we or are we not allies? Do I not protect you and expect you to protect me—except in my covert operations? Terrorists, I have to reiterate, are at war with all of us, and if a terrorist outrage is to subject a guilty terrorist to the death penalty, how can it be limited by the nationality of his target?

If I seem to feel strongly about this issue it is because this chapter is about *prevention*. And how the hell do you prevent only those terrorist acts that are going to end up in American deaths? All those young men and women being trained in Libya and Syria and Iran have all of us as random targets.

ONE OF THE best weapons we have against terrorism is the Wiesbaden computer called "The Komissar." It is manned by a staff of several thousand working for the *Bundeskriminalt,* the West German equivalent of the FBI. It stores every clue we have about terrorists and the like: names, pseudonyms, addresses, individual movements, contacts, safe houses, appearance, disguises worn, false passports used, habits, scars, you name it. The computer in Wiesbaden is even capable of analyzing handwriting and identifying the writer in 99.6% of all cases. When a recorded voice print of a specific terrorist is available, the computer can project on a screen the physiognomy that usually produces that type of voice.

The Komissar is so effective that it has provoked concern from civil liberties bodies. Those concerns, in my view, are unjustified. The computer is used to fight crime and terrorism. Although I recognize that there could be some misuse of information, at this point the benefits clearly outweigh the negatives. Unless we win the fight against terrorism—which is a priority of the computer— there won't be much in the way of civil liberties to worry about.

ALL WANTED TERRORISTS of all nationalities should have their faces, names, pseudonyms, crimes, and other vital statistics on "Wanted" posters in all post offices and other suitable public places. The West Germans tried it. They received an unusual number of tips and, with the help of this information from the public, hunted many terrorists down.

To some people such posters would be an eyesore and an uncomfortable reminder of terrorism. My answer is that if you are uncomfortable seeing their faces and knowing their crimes, perhaps your discomfort will inspire a selfish need to help get rid of the problem.

THE ERADICATION OF terrorism by preventive measures cannot by definition be a passive affair. You cannot train rapid response teams only for response. They have to go out and find the enemy on his home ground and nail him before his next strike. To watch a good example of preventive action at work, let's take a look at the German GSG9.

When GSG9 was first formed in response to the Munich fiasco, it consisted of some ninety "investigators" who were organized into small teams. Each team was given the job of learning everything it could about a single terrorist. It is amazing how a small amount of information about a terrorist's habits can lead to weaving a net in which he will be caught.

One man may have a certain woman friend in Wiesbaden whom he usually telephones from the airport or from a public phone. A wiretap on her phone is expensive to maintain but pays off handsomely, for it is the most reliable means of knowing that this terrorist has arrived in town. Wiesbaden is in the midst of a number of NATO-nation military complexes. If a terrorist is in Wiesbaden, it could spell serious trouble. By means of the phone tap, his location is known quickly and preventive action can be taken.

Terrorists don't have friends just in sensitive cities. They can have a mother or father they keep in touch with who lives in an area where there are no sensitive installations. But a tap on the mother's or father's phone line enables GSG9 to locate *him*. A map of the cities he travels in and calls from can provide clues to his later route and intentions. GSG9's team methods of intensive knowledge of a single terrorist can be especially valuable if the terrorist

travels around Europe. Many do. One team tracked four
terrorists who were friends to a resort in Bulgaria in June
1978. The four—one male and three females—were picked
up by heavily armed German counterterrorists and spirited to a nearby airport where, not coincidentally, a Lufthansa plane was waiting. These weren't small fish. The
man, Till Meyer, had escaped from a maximum security
prison four weeks earlier. He had been awaiting trial for
the kidnaping of the Christian Democrat leader of West
Berlin, Peter Lorenz. More important, eleven other major
terrorists were successfully closed in on and captured during the same brief period in 1978 by GSG9's team method.

Civil libertarians, who sometimes do not see society as a
balance of the rights of individuals, will inevitably object
loudly about abductions of fugitives in foreign countries.
They lack a sense of history.

American Senator Arlen Specter of Pennsylvania, in
early 1986, won unanimous backing in the Senate for his
"Terrorist Prosecution Act," a flawed bill in that it deals
with terrorist acts only against Americans. The bill would
make it a crime for anyone to attack, wound, or kill an
American citizen anywhere. Not being an American, as I
have said, I would like to see such bills broadened to
include the rest of us, and also to permit the extradition of
terrorists *from* America if a foreign government wants to
bring them to trial.

In any event, when Senator Specter encounters legalistic objections to picking up suspects abroad for trial in the
United States, he is fond of citing the case of Frederick M.
Ker. A century ago Ker, who was charged with embezzle-
ment and larceny in the Chicago area, took refuge in, of all
places, Lima, Peru. An American agent seized him in Peru
and caused his involuntary return to the United States. He
was brought to trial in Cook County, Illinois, and convicted. Ker sued the state of Illinois, and the case went
before the Supreme Court of the United States. The
Supreme Court upheld his conviction even though Ker had

been brought back to the United States from another country by force.

So much for legalistic objectors who rely on precedent.

Naturally, one would prefer that the democratic nations would agree to extradite terrorists when legally constituted courts in the countries where they have committed crimes demand their return for trial. The problem arises because some countries choose to call terrorist crimes "political" and therefore prevent the legal extradition of terrorists on the grounds that they are "political refugees." That is where attitudes have to be changed and the air cleared. A political refugee is someone who is escaping from a government that wants his head because he is a political opponent or because it wants to punish him for his ethnic background. That definition doesn't fit a terrorist. I don't know of any definition of "political refugee" that would include terrorists, who are international killers whom all countries ought to abhor and want to see brought to trial.

But as a counterterrorist, I cannot bear to sit twiddling my thumbs for a generation while the democratic nations play semantic games. Too many innocent lives are being lost each year, and the terrorist threat will get worse, not better, with the escalation of their weaponry. I therefore believe that if a country can't get a terrorist legally extradited, it can and should resort to the same means GSG9 used or that the U.S. Marshals used to return the terrorist arms merchant Edwin Wilson to the United States. This is particularly pertinent when a country is in hot pursuit of a terrorist. My point is that terrorists are military enemies at war with the rest of mankind. Hot pursuit of a terrorist trail across national boundaries makes absolute sense when they threaten all nations. And I especially have no compunctions about snatching them out of any country—including Iron Curtain countries, as I indicated the Germans have done—that gives terrorists safe haven or a place to have a holiday in between outrages. My priority is the civil liberties of victims, and to me, anyone who has the civil liberties of the terrorists as a priority is extremely misguided and living a life insulated from the realities of their outrages.

AS RECENTLY AS January 6, 1986, a U.S. official was claiming that there were "up to 15" terrorist training camps in Libya. To people in counterterrorist work, that is not exactly news. It is not exactly accurate either, as the terrorist camp population frequently moves not only within Libya, setting up temporary facilities, but throughout several Middle Eastern countries. As I have pointed out earlier, these camps are known and targeted.

There are no innocent bystanders in those camps. The camps are well within reach of qualified Special Forces teams available from a number of nations involved in the front line fight with terrorism. Qaddafi cannot protect the camps against such attacks on a continuing basis.

Those in government know of the covert abilities at their disposal. Those members of government who have qualms about such direct action can always derive comfort from the use of mercenaries who are deniable and can be recruited from former members of the Special Forces. In using such people, the diplomatic exposure decreases, the cost sometimes increases, but the result is the same.

It has been suggested that if Western governments officially target terrorist training camps, it gives a degree of legitimacy to the enemy. This is nonsense! What gives legitimacy to terrorists is dealing with them through diplomacy rather than through military action, thus elevating their status. Terrorists rejoice in and exploit Western diplomatic moves to appease them and to try to negotiate with them. Terrorists love to use prolonged negotiation. Publicity is a primary objective.

For those who oppose taking out the terrorist training camps, let me remind you that terrorists have always held the initiative. They have chosen where, how, and when to strike. They use surprise to the maximum. If they tire of killing innocent people in crowds at airports and other public places, they can go after oil pipelines, power lines, and nuclear plants. They can poison reservoirs, blow up trains, subways, and assassinate heads of state. In addition to their training facilities, these camps have been used to hold hostages (a French television crew was taken in March 1986 to such a camp in the Bekaa Valley in Lebanon).

A raid on terrorist camps in Libya or Lebanon by professionals would be less destructive of civilian life than retaliatory bombing raids and less expensive than using the Sixth Fleet in the Mediterranean. The preoccupation of the Sixth Fleet with terrorism must be viewed by the Soviets with some amusement.

Qaddafi is not the only benefactor of terrorism, but he must be dealt with sooner rather than later. He is training a whole generation of high school students, as part of their curriculum, to use terrorist weapons. He is inspiring the students with hatred and a goal of world revolution. The students are indoctrinated in the belief that America and her allies are their target.

A successful elimination of the terrorist training camps in Libya and the Lebanon would, I predict, not only prevent a generation of replacements but also undermine the power of both Qaddafi in Libya and Assad in Syria. Such raids carried out successfully would also make homeless a good number of European terrorists presently training or acting as instructors in the camps.

It is an absolute red herring to suggest that a Special Forces action would incur the chance of another Vietnam quagmire. The whole point of such actions is to get in and get out, as my team and I did in Beirut, or as the SAS did in the Iranian Embassy in London, or GSG9 at Mogadishu, or the Israelis in Entebbe, or the American Special Forces in the Son Tay raid in 1970.

INTELLIGENCE CHANNELS ARE now getting a good deal of information not only from graduates of the terrorist training camps who have been captured and interrogated over a period of time; interesting information vital in planning attacks is also coming from inside the camps, more than two-thirds of which have been infiltrated by Arabs and Europeans who are working for the intelligence services.

The Israelis have been especially proficient in the long-term training of foreign nationals who are helped to develop Arab contacts, sometimes through carefully contrived love affairs, that eventually get the agent infiltrated into a terrorist training camp in the guise of someone with strong sympathies for the terrorist movement who wants to help the cause. The terrorists who run these camps are, of course, not fools, and they have set up elaborate cutouts and other security measures to prevent easy access to the camps by ostensible friends until they have a chance to prove themselves. The Palestinians are particularly cautious and never let their guard down. They tend to regard all strangers as strangers even when they act as friends.

Nevertheless, I have personal knowledge of instances in which patient and resourceful Israeli intelligence work has gotten people into the camps and information out identifying terrorist leaders and future plans. At times, this information has been of sufficient importance to encourage the Israelis to share the intelligence with its allies. That, of course, is a risky business, considering the number of Soviet spies who have been exposed among the Americans and British alone. Information about infiltration that gets to the Soviets is passed down, usually through the GRU (Soviet Army Intelligence) in the Soviet Embassy in Athens to Syrian, Libyan, or PLO representatives and then on to the terrorists. More than one infiltrator has been cut down by such leakage. Nevertheless, people with guts keep getting into the secret camps, and information keeps coming out.

To be perfectly realistic, all countries have their own self-interest at heart. Americans have been known to con-

ceal intelligence information from their British allies
when they had doubts about British security, and the same
is true of the British when they had doubts about America's leaks. Self-interest dictates that a country give as little
as possible, for a secret shared is no longer a secret. The
problem is that such a policy of self-interest works against
the needs of counterterrorist special forces, which must
have access to as much information about a given target or
operation as possible, no matter from what source.

Israel, for instance, has good intelligence sources from
its operators in other countries. It shares this information
with its allies, but often reluctantly, and almost always
with some calculation of what advantages might be
obtained in return.

ONE SOURCE OF information about the terrorist camps is
not from inside but from on high. The intelligence satellites that provided us with clear pictures of Soviet missile
sites in Cuba have given us the evidence we need not only
of the existence of the terrorist training camps in Libya,
Syria, and Iran, but of their precise location and the size of
their floating population as well.

Spy satellites and the technology they have on board
allow us to look into the camps and make the most detailed
reconnaissance, courtesy of the highly secret National
Reconnaissance Office (NRO). This agency, operating
from the nether regions of the Pentagon, controls America's spy satellites. The "product" of its surveillance is
shared with Britain's MI6 and selected agencies of other
friendly nations.

With the first satellites, information was stored on film
and then ejected every few days to descend by parachute
over the Pacific. The canisters of film were snared out of
the sky by specially equipped aircraft, and then flown to
Hawaii for analysis. The "Big Bird" and KH-8 satellites
employing this technique continue to give valuable service. Unbelievably, their recording capabilities make pos-

sible the reading of a newspaper headline from seventy miles up. But the information is not "real time," on-the-spot reconnaissance.

We now have orbiting the earth, at an altitude of between 160 and 300 miles, the KH-11 (KEYHOLE) satellite. The ability of this fourteen-ton, truck-sized piece of spaceware is one example of what can be put at the disposal of the forces of counterterrorism. On command, it can be dropped down to an altitude of 100 miles and directed over the terrorist camp or operational area being targeted. Its camera, with a focal length of twenty feet, is switched on and immediately begins to transmit what it is seeing to computers in Washington. This is done not by film, but by the use of millions of light sensitive diodes translating the intensity of light being received into digital impulses. The impulses are transmitted through a relay satellite over the Atlantic to Washington, where computers convert them back into light and into the eagerly awaited television pictures. The reconnaissance detail required for the operational briefing is then extracted and dispatched in video or still-shot form. Once the satellite is positioned properly, probably the longest time segment of the operation is the seven minutes it takes for the pictures to be taken by helicopter from the Pentagon to the Task Room at the White House across the Potomac River.

I have attended briefings that have included such reconnaissance, and the television picture viewed is of a sharp focus and definition, far superior to that on a domestic television set. The ability to freeze frame and "click down" until it is possible to tell whether a man is bearded or unbearded, never fails to amaze me.

Even more amazing is the fact that what you see happening on the roof of a house in Beirut, or in a terrorist training camp off the road between Tripoli and Bengazi in Libya, is less than one hour old.

The United States also has "Ferret" satellites that can eavesdrop on long distance calls and radio traffic. This

means that the Americans can provide the counterterrorist forces of their allies with up-to-the-minute sound reconnaissance that is invaluable just before a mission is
launched.

IT IS NOT only the training camps that need to be taken out
of action, but also the safe havens provided for terrorists
who have already been trained. They are scattered all over
the Middle East and Europe. The location of many are
known. Other locations can be ascertained through offered
rewards and through interrogation. Safe houses within
these safe havens have to be made unsafe. And as new safe
houses are set up, as soon as intelligence information gives
us their location they need to be hit by quick in-and-out
counterterrorist squads. The war has to be taken to the
enemy. Nobody ever bested a fanatical enemy by sitting in
an armchair and waiting for his next strike.

ONE AMERICAN-BORN woman who had the right mind-set
was Golda Meir. She immigrated to Israel and in due
course became prime minister some years before Margaret
Thatcher ascended to the same high office in Britain.
Once, in a heated debate in the Israeli Parliament, she
characterized a policy of prevention perfectly when she
said, "We killed the murderers who were planning to kill
again."

In May 1978, while attending a weapons firing demonstration on the outskirts of Madrid, I was introduced to the
Argentinian commodore who had been given the task of
solving Argentina's terrorist problem.

The reader will remember that in the 1960s a terrorist
group called the Monteneros swept up literally millions of
dollars in kidnap ransom. The Monteneros presented
themselves with a typical appeal: they were robbing the
rich to feed the poor. They, along with the People's Revolutionary Army (ERP), turned kidnapping into a major
industry. Unfortunately, and not unexpectedly, the work-

ing class poor saw very little of the vast sums these terrorists obtained through kidnapping, occasional random
murder to underline their "seriousness," and extortion.
These activities were on a scale that began to undermine
foreign confidence in Argentina's ability to protect itself
against the terrorists, and the result had an impact on the
entire Argentinian economy.

During the course of our conversation, the commodore
said that the only foreign nationals who reacted properly
to the crisis in Argentina were the British, who hired ex-
SAS members from a London firm dealing in their services, and posted them to guard the British Embassy and
its personnel with orders to shoot to kill.

"And the Monteneros and ERP?" I asked.

Long years at the sharp end of antiterrorist work had
given the commodore a particularly taciturn expression.
At my question, he shrugged his shoulders. "They no
longer exist. They were eliminated."

Message received.

TODAY, KIDNAPPING FOR ransom is old hat, and murder is
in. A cross-Europe terrorist alliance, as I have indicated,
now has a stated policy of carrying out selective assassinations.

Ernst Zimmerman was an important German indus-
trialist who shrugged his shoulders about terrorism and
took no particular precautions about his own safety. On
February 1, 1985, a male/female Red Army Faction terrorist team tied up Zimmerman in his own home and executed
him. His death had a major impact in West Germany.
Businessmen who, like Zimmerman, had shrugged their
shoulders in a fatalistic view of the terrorist danger,
started taking precautionary measures for the first time.

It is not only businessmen who are targets. On March 27,
1985 the Italian Red Brigades killed Ezio Tarantelli, a
labor union economist. Public figures are targets. Diplomatic personnel are targets. And in airports and on planes,

in cafes and arcades, everywhere that people gather in groups, everyone is a target.

The terrorists have given us the option of living our lives out barricaded like eccentrics in our homes, spending billions on precautions that the terrorists will learn to outwit, or taking the initiative and eliminating the terrorists by the use of special forces and law enforcement dedicated to the role of counterterrorism.

Is there really a choice?

13

The Strategy and Tactics of Winning

The Universal Declaration of Human Rights, promulgated by the United Nations, says everyone has the right to life and "security of the person" and that "no one shall be arbitrarily deprived of his life." Tell that to the terrorists. The fact is that terrorists are in the business of arbitrarily depriving people of their lives. Counterterrorists are in the business of depriving terrorists of *their* lives—but *not* arbitrarily.

The role of the United Nations is to provide a safe platform in the diplomatic arena for all member nations to discuss issues and thus avoid any conflict that might arise through misunderstanding. The theory is that while nations are talking, they are not fighting. As Churchill put it so succinctly, "Jaw-jaw is better than war-war." It is a valid theory, which I support. The fact that all members of the United Nations cynically use it on occasions to advance self-interest is just a fact of life.

Whenever the United Nations ventures outside the diplomatic arena, however, it usually does so with disastrous results. A string of impotent policing actions has complicated many conflicts as far apart as the Congo and Lebanon. Any declaration issued by that body, however, does set the standard and in most situations lays out the rules—or at least their parameters.

Those of us in the front line who have learned to watch terrorists either scoff at the Declaration of Human Rights or, when convenient, shelter behind it. Thus, to the counter-terrorist, that high-sounding declaration becomes just another piece of paper that perhaps helps the politician to sleep at nights but that has no significance in the shooting war.

Terrorism is multinational and demands a multinational response. The carrying out of an effective and aggressive policy demands the close cooperation of counterterrorist operators, intelligence networks, and politicians worldwide. The United Nations should provide the ideal platform for that common ground, the opening up of national borders and air space in a quick response to any terrorist action. In reality, that policy does not work, for amongst the U.N. members are those very nations who support terrorism.

And there are also such U.N. countries as Greece and its well-known airport at Athens. Terrorist activity from this Mediterranean launching pad is rampant, and Athens is viewed as perhaps one of the most dangerous aerial crossroads in the world. A recent Russian defector named Bokhan, who was attached to the Soviet Embassy in Athens from 1968 to 1975 and was a member of the GRU, confirmed that the GRU was orchestrating terrorist acts both in Greece and abroad with the aim of creating subversion and terror worldwide.

The GRU is the Soviet directorate of army intelligence and operates quite independently of the KGB. In addition to intelligence and subversive activity, it has within its ranks units that could be compared with Western special forces and which function as assassination teams, commandoes, and instructors. Perhaps as a result of Bokhan's

revelations, in late 1985 the Greek leader Andreas Papan-
dreou announced the arrest on terror charges of a member
of the Greek State Intelligence Service. It must have been a
somewhat reluctant arrest, as his activities have been
known to European counterterrorist agencies for some
time.

However, this has not resulted in a cleanup and a cutting
out of the terrorist mechanism. Intelligence shows that the
Greek terror group N170 has been directed by Qaddafi to
ease off their terrorist efforts while a substantial arms deal
has been transacted between Libya and Greece. Further,
in November 1985 the Soviet representative in Athens,
Igor Andropov, son of the late Soviet leader, was replaced
by Vladimir Pushkin. That gentleman, a senior member of
the GRU, was expelled from the United Kingdom in 1971
for carrying out espionage.

WITH THE UNITED Nations unsuitable as a place to discuss
and agree on the defeat of terrorism, counterterrorism has
led to the creation of other forums. There are some at a
political level, such as the Kilowatt Group, and the Club of
Berne to which the controllers of the democratic secret
intelligence services belong. Though not members of the
European Economic Community, Israel and Switzerland
are members. The only EEC country that does not belong
is the Republic of Ireland. The club provides for the exchange of current information at a high level, and appropriate data is filtered through to operational levels. Of
equal priority are the overall strategy and the appropriate
tactics, which are discussed during meetings of the club.

At more operational levels, invaluable exchanges take
place among members of the special forces and special
antiterrorist police units. A typical forum for such exchanges is the AIBTI Association. (In English, those
initials stand for the International Association of Bomb
Technicians and Investigators.) Its members are at the
sharp end, handling the bombs and explosive devices

placed by terrorists and the lunatic fringe in all parts of the world daily. The bomb data centers, operating in London and as faraway as South Africa, Israel, America, and Australia, glean vital information from every device encountered. The bomber's technique and his favorite components become his signature and often provide the evidence of links between terrorist groups.

All of this is vital in the war against terrorism, but the selfless work carried out by these forces is, as we have observed, so often thwarted by courtroom charades and governments handing captured terrorists their freedom—as in the case of Italy and Mohammed Abbas in the *Achille Lauro* affair.

The dumping of terrorists elsewhere, along with the problem they represent, is dangerous short-term thinking and is not unlike the American practice of deporting convicted Mafia leaders back to Italy. That action served to complicate the Mafia's communications logistics but solved no problems for the United States. The Mafia leaders merely continued to operate their rackets in the States from Italy.

To link all the present expertise in counterterrorism and to overcome the problems and complications of political sensitivity, an international umbrella organization at the highest level has to be established. Its role should be to fight terrorism and afford its member countries the unconditional protection of all the joint forces at its disposal. There will be differing levels of experience and operational readiness among the member countries, but this can be compensated for by drawing on the specialty required from within the total group. Most countries presently cooperating against terrorism have a long way to go to reach the training levels of the SAS in close-quarter combat and even further to go in becoming as experienced as the British, Israelis, and Germans are in fighting urban terrorism. The British, because of that long colonial involvement in different environments, have the undisputed lead in fighting many kinds of terrorism. Their experience extends from the jungles of Borneo to the deserts of the Arabian Gulf and to the streets of Belfast.

Just as the British are the leaders in hands-on techniques, so the Israelis are preeminent in the intelligence field. Both have gained enormous experience through their separate but long and bloody involvement in fighting persistent terrorism over the years. The technology available from America in electronic intelligence gathering and logistical support in air and sea mobility is second to none.

There is no room in the terrorist war for disruptive national pride or "soldier ego." Experience must be the decisive factor. If the individual country does not possess a "home grown" ability, it must import it from another country that does. Arab pride got in the way in the Malta hijacking, and cost lives. I have worked and trained with Arabs on their own soil, and their pride has been a source of furious inner strength for them; but that same pride in the sudden slashing exposure brought about by a terrorist crisis can bring disaster.

THERE STILL REMAIN large and widespread obstacles to international cooperation in counterterrorism. When the leader of Italy's Christian Democrat party, Aldo Moro, was kidnaped by terrorists, the Italian Government turned to the United States for special surveillance equipment that it needed. The United States refused on the specious grounds that the Red Brigades, who were being pursued by the Italians, were *domestic* terrorists and therefore the United States could not get involved. Anybody, having read my chapter on networking, will realize how ludicrous that was.

Aldo Moro was murdered in cold blood. He was an extremely popular statesman in Italy. His death was keenly felt. I do not think the United States would make such an error today, and I hope that when Mohammed

Abul Abbas flew off to Yugoslavia, a few consciences in Washington were jolted.

The French Government has an appalling record of compromising in the fight against terrorists. I have already mentioned several times the safe haven given to the Basque ETA terrorists. Europe—including France itself—is still suffering from President Mitterand's clemency to French terrorists in 1981, and the Arab groups consider France a soft touch. Two examples will suffice.

The French police arrested a man named Wilfried Bose, who was an associate of the notorious terrorist Carlos. As he was a German, his deportation was eagerly awaited by the Federal German Border Guard. But the French drove him to the German border unannounced and let him go. Bose was next heard from when he led the mixed Arab-European terrorist team that hijacked the Air France airbus to Entebbe.

France is learning the errors of its ways. It is coming, I hope, to realize the cold fact that you can never gain by ingratiating yourself with the terrorists.

On December 19, 1971, a terrorist named Frazeh Khaelfa attempted to kill the Jordanian Ambassador to London, Zaid el Rifia. At the junction of Campden Hill Road and Duchess of Bedford's Walk, West, in London, Khaelfa riddled the Ambassador's Daimler with a Sten gun. The Ambassador's driver accelerated the car to safety, with the Ambassador sustaining a bullet wound only in his right hand. Khaelfa made his escape in a waiting car driven by an accomplice. With luck, Khaelfa was arrested in the French city of Lyons, having been successfully assisted out of Britain by his Arab accomplices. The British issued a warrant for attempted murder and pleaded to have Khaelfa extradited so that he could be tried in the British courts. The Lyons court recommended that Khaelfa be deported to London. The French Ministry of Foreign Affairs turned its back on its British allies, ignored the French court ruling, and released Khaelfa on a technicality. He traveled in comfort to Algeria and to a victorious welcome.

WITHIN COUNTRIES THE bureaucratic attachment to the chain of command is another major obstacle to building an effective national counterterrorist force—one that is flexible enough to respond as a whole or act as a part of an international force. The chains of command might more accurately be described as the chains of bureaucracy. Of course, just as in any large corporation, the military must have a command structure. But many successful large corporations have learned to delegate authority down to line managers, whereas military authorities often lag behind in this regard. Everything has to be done "by the numbers" through the regular and recognized channels, up to the man who makes the decision and back down again to the individual who requires it. Checks and balances must exist, but they have been the frustration of many a vital operation. Fine tuning must be applied to achieve a safe and rapid response to a terrorist outrage.

The American Delta Force, on which America pins its counterterrorist hopes, is upgrading its abilities all the time. But it has suffered costly setbacks and has lost good men, partly because of the system in which it operates. In the early days of the SAS, the men who made up this elite regiment had to fight for its very survival against bureaucratic intransigence and jealousies brought on by the chain of command. Unfortunately, there is in human nature an envy of elitism—even in the armed forces. Delta Force has been a victim of the same human failing although its command has resisted to good effect. But higher office has to stomp on any petty interference that slows the development of Delta and its Navy SEAL equivalent.

I know of one instance not so long ago in which a Delta team was deployed in response to a hijacking. It had been lifted by helicopter to an offshore naval vessel in close combat order. It was a self-contained unit, primed for action and ready to go in. Its task was already defined, and the team had been fully briefed. The ship was to serve as vital transport and to occupy a standoff position. Once it boarded the ship, the assault team came under the command of the ship's captain. Naturally, there was a big difference in rank between the leader of the assault team and the ship's captain. The latter, who also had a wider command role in the fleet, felt that he should, as his right, assume command over the assault team. His expertise lay in operating his ship and placing the assault team in its predetermined launch position. That was a vital role affecting the mission, but its function was logistical and naval, not one of counterterrorism and assault. What resulted was a clash of personalities and role-playing— and the sad consequence was that the assault team was totally undermined. This kind of situation always creates mission failures.

Priority must be given to recognizing that interagency and interservice rivalry exists, and any task force commander must have a clear mandate to override it. The inherent dangers of this rivalry court the very failure of an operation. I have personally witnessed its cost of lives, and it has been publicly demonstrated in the disastrous results at Desert One during the American hostage rescue attempt in Iran.

It is absolutely crucial that a rapid response operation remain an autonomous force with a direct communications link to whatever command group holds the final authority to give the "Go" signal. Equally crucial, the assault team commander must never suffer any peripheral distraction. He should not be deluged with unnecessary contact or intelligence feedback not directly sent by the intelligence liaison officer specially assigned to the mission. That liaison officer is vital in the final countdown phase of the assault. The whole mass of unrelated intelligence facts from various sources flood in to the intelligence liaison officer, who has the major task of separating the immediate and important (as far as the assault team is concerned) from all other data. Thus, he sifts the vital elements from all the intelligence-gathering and passes only the details essential to the assault team in clipped voice communication or coded burst transmission via satellite in a continual update, thus eliminating delay and confusion. Sadly, many counterterrorist actions today are still hampered by unnecessary bureaucratic confusion.

During the Entebbe raid the Israelis showed outstandingly how quick and accurate decisions can only be taken on the basis of good and up-to-date intelligence information. In Israel, the general with overall command of the operation stood shoulder to shoulder with the President of Israel as he talked by long-range radio to the colonel commanding the task group. Thus both the civil and military powers were as one, and the task group commander had the great benefit of receiving up-to-date information minute by minute. It worked wonderfully well, but we must perhaps bear in mind that Israel is a small and democratic country, and a sense of companionship in the common cause is solidly developed.

Let us now examine the British method, which I consider to be ideal. A good example is the attack on the Iranian Embassy in London on May 6, 1980. This brought into operation COBRA (Cabinet Office Briefing Room). This command cell is chaired by the Home Secretary of the day, who reports directly to the Prime Minister. The group includes a junior minister from the Departments of Defense and Foreign Affairs respectively, advisors representing the police, MI5, and the SAS. Should the crisis warrant it, a representative of MI6 would be present. (MI5 handles counterintelligence within the United Kingdom, whereas MI6 procures international intelligence.)

Thus the SAS assault team has a direct link to these decision makers and operational links to the police. We must not forget that this particular example, the assault on the Iranian Embassy, took place in a major city. It is only as a last resort that the police hand over their duties to the military—and only when the final decision to take military action has been made by COBRA. At this point, the officer commanding the police operation formally hands the area and command over to the military commander. From that point until its measured conclusion, the action is wholly a military one.

As the world saw on its television screens, the Iranian Embassy seige was resolved with speed and control. As the operation progressed, vital information was passing between the SAS officer in charge of the assault team, the police, and COBRA. During the assault through the building, there was constant radio communication between each member of the team and the commander, which in turn was being picked up by the chief of police and COBRA in Whitehall. Anyone privileged to be listening in on the radio network would have heard a running commentary on the lines of "Room A, two terrorists, two terrorists dead, proceeding up staircase, one terrorist at head of stairs, one terrorist dead, telex room cleared, one dead, hostages located in Room C, all safe, moving them downstairs"— and so on.

The moment the action was over, command was formally returned to the police, and the SAS discreetly withdrew. The COBRA group then dispersed, I daresay with the hope that they would not be meeting each other again in similar circumstances for a very long time.

I well recall from similar operations I have taken part in, wearing a gas mask with a throat microphone, the sound of my own breath magnified in my ears, and the sweaty, confined feeling as one moves fast through a building. You feel the click of your weapon when you fire, but the report is often drowned or merged with external noises. Each member of the team, having practiced endlessly in training for this kind of assault, moves slickly, taking his targets with total confidence that another member of the team will be backing him up, just as he is backing up others. It all becomes a deadly ballet, danced at speed, but with a set choreography in the mind of each team member.

In the relief of the Iranian Embassy seige, every step was confined to the immediate area of the embassy. Outside, the world went on as always, and the government could conduct other affairs of state, having delegated responsibility for the operation to a tightly knit and highly motivated task force. The public was protected as the crisis demanded. The whole operation can be summed up in one word—efficient.

Behind the scenes of this crisp operation was the mindset I spoke of earlier. There was clear knowledge from the start that once the decision had been taken to hand the operation over to the military, they would go in and finish the job—their prime task being the safety of the hostages. If that meant killing all the terrorists involved, so be it. Mercy to a terrorist comes a distant second to protecting innocent people who have found themselves caught up in a bizarre situation.

Behind the successful operation that appeared on TV screens, the right kind of logistical support was essential. Long SAS experience has proved the vital need for special forces to have their own transport, including helicopters, under their direct control and on call at any time. They also have the ability to acquire needed equipment without delay.

THE AMERICANS LEARNED after the Teheran operation that logistics, transport, and equipment procurement could not be taken for granted. I firmly believe that the objectives in Teheran were achievable as a special forces operation. The individual Delta members whom I know personally were quite capable of doing the right thing had they got there. They were let down by the wrong mission concept, bad planning, and, quite frankly, by too many people trying to muscle in on the act.

After the failure of the mission was analyzed, a special concept and logistics group, given the title of Joint Special Operations Command—or as it is more commonly known, JAYSOC—was created. The group was headed by a major general, whose task was to work out plans to form, train, and expand the concept of operating a joint armed services counterterrorist force.

The thinking behind JAYSOC was wrong from the outset. It has no command authority over the dispersed elements included in its assignment. It receives no priority for obtaining the right equipment from the monolithic procurement structure of the U.S. armed forces. Let me give an example. I demonstrated some special equipment and showed the training methods for its use to the evaluation unit of Delta Force. The evaluating team was highly impressed and decided, in view of a pending operation, that it required the equipment very urgently. The JAYSOC officer present was equally in favor but, because of the massive bureaucracy prevailing in the U.S. armed forces, all his efforts were in vain. Eventually, after all the red tape and form-filling had been completed, the equipment probably would have been made available—but by then it would have been far too late for the operation in question.

This problem is by no means unique to the Americans but is exaggerated by the sheer size of the U.S. defense procurement system. On numerous occasions, I have taken the frustrations of the special forces unit leaders to a colonel in the Pentagon. He applied the no-nonsense approach that I had known him for when he was a serving major in Vietnam, and he managed to get around the system to accommodate the urgency. On occasion, he even carried some of the man-portable equipment to Fort Bragg himself.

The elements under JAYSOC include the Army's Special Force Delta, located at Fort Bragg, North Carolina; Task Force 160, a high-speed helicopter unit stationed at Fort Campbell, Kentucky; the Navy's SEAL (Sea-Air-

Land) team; 6 counterterrorist Units at Norfolk, Virginia; a very proficient underwater demolition and frogman assault unit, and a specialized air force wing based at Eglin Air Force base in Florida. That wing operates Lockheed Hercules C-130 aircraft equipped for counterterrorist operations.

JAYSOC, without an autonomous command structure, is fragmented, cumbersome, without centralized planning or training. Interservice rivalry persists. In peacetime that may be fair sport, but in the terrorist war there is no intermission.

Crisis can strike any time, and readiness is the key. Any period between crises has to be devoted to continuous training to insure that readiness. I have seen a team training for a predicted operation suddenly come up with a revised technique that might improve the result. They spent endless time trying to requisition the helicopter they now found they needed. What a waste. It should have been outside on the ramp.

With the huge resources of the United States, it is alarming that this state of affairs exists. President Reagan has declared his aim of defeating terrorism—and now it is up to him to shake the bureaucracy out of the way. It is already late in the day. The color of the uniform must be of no consequence; the special skill of the man or unit has to be the criterion. Budgets that allow the evaluation units in these special forces to buy and experiment with the latest "state of the art" counterterrorist equipment must be put into effect at once. If the equipment is determined to be suitable and necessary, then the appropriate requisition to purchase it should at once be put on a desk in the Pentagon dedicated to the counterterrorist function. The system has to respond because this war erupts again and again without warning.

I recall Colonel Charles Beckwith coming to Europe before the Teheran raid. He had a good idea of what equipment was needed for the job, and he had the checkbook in his pocket. I received an order on his behalf for equipment essential for the assault had they reached the embassy. The urgency dictated immediate delivery, and I personally took the equipment to the U.S. Embassy in London. A special forces major serving there at the time was acting as liaison officer for Colonel Beckwith, who had returned to the States. A U.S. Army colonel, who happened to be visiting the attaché's office, asked what was going on. When told, he pulled rank and uttered the immortal phrase that the U.S. Embassy in London was "no goddam purchasing office" for Beckwith. He overrode the major and ordered that established procedures must be followed. In other words, the purchase order had to be physically sent to Washington and go through channels. Fort Bragg never did get the equipment. There is an American word that aptly describes this type of—shall we say—bullheaded behavior. I'll just say I found it unbelievable in the circumstances.

THE DIFFERENT SITUATIONS that can arise anywhere in the world at the whim of the terrorist require that our reaction time be reduced to the minimum. This further requires that special forces' teams, their prepared equipment, and transport be strategically placed in relation to predicted terrorist operations. The pattern of terrorist activity over an extended period allows those locations to be accurately pinpointed. The criteria for selecting the locations is the time it takes for aircraft or ships to reach points within a given radius. Some choice is then available to the task force commander as to how he delivers his assault team to the target and the method of the assault itself.

Ultimately, I would hope that a multinational response would be possible. When a crisis erupts, the head of state of whatever country is the unfortunate host will at once initiate a response and link into the cellular task force structure, calling on the best expertise available from the member nations closest at hand. If an aircraft or ship of another nation is involved or if there happen to be foreign nationals on board that aircraft or that ship, then the head of state of the respective countries must be automatically involved and become directly linked to the command structure.

This kind of crisis management by pre-agreed consent will eliminate much of the hesitancy that characterizes present-day crises. The decision to take military action, or at the least to move to a standby position, should be done with the confidence that the assault teams are of the highest available standard.

In my opinion, that standard can be no less than equal to the SAS, and the combat swim-and-underwater demolition component should be equal to the standards demanded by the SBS (Special Boats Squadron) or the U.S. Navy SEALs. These teams would train to be coopted as necessary as a unit or as individuals, linked to the other units in the alliance.

Any member head of state should have a mandate to initiate the action of the international response team in a hostage crisis. This would help cut out fiascos like that of the Egyptair plane in Malta. Not only were the Maltese incapable of responding, they dragged their heels and blocked any chance of effective action. Their position was further confused by their links to Libya.

Egypt, as a member of the counterterrorist alliance, would not have felt compelled to use an ill-trained assault force, nor felt intimidated about calling for help. There is no loss of face if calling on the units of other nations is a part of the pre-agreed plan.

To improve the mobility of the response teams and to allow them to be formed up and transported rapidly, equipment containers should be located in pre-selected places such as strategically situated military bases and secure international airports. The containers should be customized to allow them to be uplifted by mid- to long-distance transport, such as the Sikorsky HH-53C and Boeing Chinook CH-47 helicopters and Hercules C130 aircraft. They will be prepacked for specific operations so that when the team members and the appropriate containers rendezvous, it is a matter of opening up the containers, selecting and donning the kit, and going to work. The procedure is the same whether it takes place over the Mediterranean in the belly of a C130 with the assault team preparing to jump, or on the ground a short helicopter ride from the target.

The use of units like the American Air Force's 67th ARRS (Aerospace Rescue and Recovery Squadron), quartered at the Royal Air Force base at Woodbridge in England, is also essential. This unique unit, with three overseas detachments, two of which are desirably close for the counterterrorist role (at Ramstein air base, central Germany, and Zaragoza, Spain), would make a major contribution. Its headquarters flying group at Woodbridge consists of five C130 Hercules Transports and five of the huge Sikorsky HH-53C-type helicopters, which are similar to the naval type Sea Stallions used in the Teheran raid. Its squadron personnel are extremely highly skilled in pararescue and combat SAR (Search and Rescue), and they maintain a state of readiness that allows them to launch a combat mission within thirty minutes as well as being fully prepared to deploy to forward operating locations (FOLs).

ARRS is also trained in the very special skills of low-level transport of special forces operatives. But it is the added characteristics of the aircraft's configuration that supply the unique benefits. The big HH-53C helicopters are equipped with self-sealing fuel tanks and armor plating, which offer protection against a small arms ground fire. They also include an external hoist with 250 feet of cable and three 7.62-mm machine guns each. The machine guns are manned by the flight mechanic and two pararescue men during combat. Another unique asset is the fact that the HH-53C helicopters are fitted with a retractable inflight refueling probe that extends their nonstop range beyond anything in its class. The squadron has been known to carry out a nonstop flight from the southern tip of Italy to the Woodbridge base in England in just over nine hours. With an instrument system that gives it an all-weather capability and the capacity to carry many men at high speed, the combination is invaluable.

With its great range and flexibility in special forces helicopter operations and its ability to operate at night, the HH-53C and the Chinook CH-47D (which is also equipped for inflight refueling and has night vision capability) are useful ingredients in any counterterrorist arsenal.

The 67th ARSS is typical of the unique resources available to the United States. Adding this squadron to a rapid-response counterterrorist group would bring a marked increase in its effectiveness.

I believe a highly mobile force must train together and attain a uniformly high standard across its ranks. It should have a ready interface with the various law enforcement agencies. The intelligence data from computer operations, such as the German Kommisar and the new Irish MIRIAM system (based on a similar British system), must be integrated into the net. Cross-indexing of the available information on all terrorist suspects and their associates must also be part of the net. Individual terrorists must be identified in as great detail as possible, and their every move, when learned, fed into the computer network as an update. It is the results of detective work, fed into the computer net, that is one of the strengths of the counterterrorist effort. The secret strength, of course, is the information that flows into the net from undercover operatives inside the countries that sponsor terrorism and from the very camps where terrorists are being trained.

When international cooperation against terrorism is put into place, some of the more hesitant nations will take their lead from the stronger ones. Had such an environment existed over the last decade and a half, examples of individual strength would have rubbed off on others. Israel would not have been left to soul-search on its own after the post-Munich hit team was recalled, the Spanish success would have spilled over into British and German efforts against their respective terrorist threats, and the earlier example of Prime Minister Trudeau of Canada would have gotten its rightful recognition.

As a case in point, Canada, an amalgam of citizens of British and French extraction, has long had a French-separatist movement that in itself may be legitimate as a political enterprise, but that became illegitimate when it began to employ terrorist methods. The late sixties saw an ugly blossoming of attacks. In October 1970, French Canadian separatists kidnapped the British Trade Commissioner of Quebec, James Cross. The terrorists demanded half a million dollars, and, more significantly, that Prime Minister Trudeau release members of the group already jailed. Trudeau adopted a hard line of not giving in to the terrorists' demands, a difficult but necessary choice in the end if terrorism is to be stopped in its tracks. The terrorists escalated the confrontation by kidnapping and killing the Quebec Minister of Labor, Pierre Laporte. The pressure on Trudeau was severe. He finally agreed to a deal. Three of the kidnappers and four of their relatives were allowed to fly to Cuba in exchange for the release of James Cross.

Trudeau did not like having his arm twisted in this way, and so in 1970 he invoked the War Measures Act. He was absolutely right because that is how terrorism must be defined—as an act of war. Trudeau put both the Canadian Army and the Royal Canadian Mounted Police to work following the trail of the organizers of the kidnappings and killing. It took more than two months of intensive police work and the rounding up of more than 300 suspects to capture the ringleaders of the FLQ *(Front du Liberation du Quebec)*. As expected, pussyfooting politicians criticized Trudeau's tough stance. His response was "There are a lot of bleeding hearts around. . . . All I can say is let them bleed."

The main point I want to make here is that Trudeau's get-tough policy resulted in getting rid of terrorism in Canada for a decade. In an international consortium of counterterrorism, the success of his tough actions would have been communicated to other countries, thus having greater effect than it did. If the object is to rid a nation of terrorism, Trudeau's actions should be studied. If the object is to rid the world of terrorism, Trudeau's methods should be learned and used, for today Canada is a land with full civil liberties for all. It is crucial for bleeding hearts to learn that it is the terrorists and the governments that back them that would deprive all the rest of us of our civil liberties, and that we have a right not to be deprived of our lives arbitrarily.

THE WORLD HAS benefited immensely in the last few decades as a result of insight and information gained from former Communists who fled the cause. Some of them have been spies or KGB operatives who have turned, providing the Western democracies with much helpful intelligence information. I don't want to get into their motivations, which may vary a great deal or never be truly known. I'm glad they were of use.

I feel the world has benefited equally from the informers, supergrasses as we call them, and the few terrorists who have deserted the cause of terrorism. Hans-Joachim Klein, who at this writing is in his late thirties, became involved with the Red Army Faction as a younger man. He met people connected with the Baader-Meinhof gang, and then the number one terrorist of his time, Carlos. He was one of Carlos's henchmen in the assault on the OPEC meeting in Vienna on December 21, 1975. Three men were shot and eleven of the oil ministers, including Sheik Yamani of Saudi Arabia and Dr. Jamshid Amouzegar of Iran, were kidnaped. Both the Arab and German terrorists wanted to kill the oil ministers, but Carlos held out for and got a $25-million ransom, not counting a $2-million gift from Qaddafi for pulling it off. Klein wasn't that lucky. He, like Carlos, was using a Beretta submachine gun. A bullet fired by a guard hit the magazine of his weapon and split into fragments that entered his stomach, causing serious injury. Qaddafi supplied $200,000 in "insurance" money for Klein to be mended—in Libya. A little more than a year later, the West German magazine *Der Spiegel* received a letter from Klein with a set of his fingerprints to prove its authenticity. The letter told of his disillusionment with terrorism. Perhaps being wounded helped. In any event, what Klein had to say about getting into the terrorist movement and why he wanted to flee is an important message to get across to would-be terrorists. Defectors can be useful *if they are used.* Long range, the recruitment of terrorists can be diminished by such efforts if handled by people who are truly experienced in the field of propaganda.

As I have already said, the "secret" international "tenmost-wanted" list of terrorists should be published openly, supplemented by a 100-next-most-wanted list, replete with photos, anatomical details, habits, etc., for display in public facilities. Newspapers should be provided with material and encouraged to publish updated photo sections of terrorists just as they, in some countries, depict weekly the faces and characteristics of missing children. A special effort might be made to have a photo gallery of the teenagers who have given their lives *uselessly* in the service of terrorist leaders who are still living. Fanatics, too, eventually succumb to the deterioration of morale experienced by members of lost causes.

WHEN THE WESTERN democracies feel really threatened they are quite capable of setting up terrific covert intelligence operations. It is no longer a secret that the real secret weapon of World War II was not the atomic bomb but

Ultra, by which I mean the organization and machines with which the British and Americans broke the Nazi codes—and the American intelligence operations that broke the Japanese codes—enabling the Allies to know what the Axis was up to every step of the way. The same war effort should now be applied to a multinational intelligence operation that is not passively collecting information but actively supplying disinformation to Libya, Syria, Iran, and the Soviet Union, specifically designed to make them distrustful of their internal security and of each other. The opportunity must be grasped to turn a liability into an advantage. I have shown the linkage among terrorist organizations worldwide. Any network composed of such disparate ethnic groupings can become a playing field for mischievous "black" intelligence. Moreover, even among the same ethnic grouping, there are opportunities to take advantage of the divisiveness, for example, among the Arabs. I am not talking about pitting the peacemakers like King Hussein against the die-hard militants. The Arabs take care of that kind of intramural warfare on their own. Within the militant majority of Arab nations, there are conflicting economic and power interests that can be exploited by covert operations. And the operation should zero in on those leaders who are most closely involved in terrorist training and operations planning. Nothing is as disorienting as distrust within one's own ranks. What the Soviets did within the British intelligence community is perfectly feasible for the West to do in the faction-ridden world of terrorism. The physical equipment is already in place that could be targeted at disrupting morale in the terrorist training camps. If cleverly handled, it could have the same effect on morale within the camps as naval bombardments have on enemy forces prior to a landing.

I TRUST THAT every reader of this book will recognize now, if he did not do so before, that terrorism is war. The terrorist knows it and is committed to it. Moreover, terrorists now have a global alliance that supersedes their original national causes. To win, countries that oppose terrorism need a global alliance that will function on behalf of any of them to seek out terrorists and destroy their training camps and their leaders, and to be ready for rapid response to a terrorist outrage when prevention fails.

International task forces are not foreign to Western democracies. One such enabled them to win the most important war of the century. If they could organize their combined strength for the invasion of a continent held by Hitler, they could organize the far fewer forces needed—an international task force of specialists, few in number, high in training—to take the initiative away from the terrorists, the benefactors who give them shelter, and the superpower that thrives on the destabilization of the West.

To give a basic idea of the shape of the mobile force in the early stages, let's have three squadrons in Europe—two operational at separate locations, and one in training, with the training rotated to keep all three squadrons up to date on equipment and techniques. An additional two squadrons in the Mediterranean—one on call, the second in training would be enough, especially since support could easily come from the European squadrons if needed. One squadron based in a friendly environment in the Middle East might substitute preventive action and provide rapid response in place of the retaliatory tit-for-tat game that has destroyed so many lives to no effect.

An additional force of four squadrons should be stationed in the United States, because of the breadth of the country and its vunerability to a terrorist attack involving several locations simultaneously. One should be based in the East, one in the Midwest, and one in the Far West (preferably in the Northwest so that Alaska would be within reach), and a fourth rotating in training at Fort Bragg. Every group in the United States should have foreign specialists attached on a rotating basis to maintain an interface with the standards and training of the squad-

rons abroad. There is plenty of precedent for this. West
Point has trained the officers of many nations, as has
Sandhurst in England. Moreover, in Vietnam the U.S. and
British Commonwealth Special Forces were frequently
merged on missions and worked effectively as teams.
When Colonel Charles Beckwith, one-time head of Delta,
was a Green Beret, he had the benefit of SAS training,
possibly the toughest in the world. In addition, the American melting pot provides people of diverse ethnic backgrounds, some who serve with U.S. intelligence, many of
whom have known terrorism in the countries they have
fled and whose languages and motivation can be useful in
counterterrorist work.

The operational squadrons should consist of twenty-five
men each. I have advocated nine squadrons, so including
those in training we are talking about 225 men. I am not
talking about armies. The United States, for instance, has
a quarter of a million soldiers in Europe whose main purpose is to prevent or counter a Soviet ground attack. Well,
the Soviets are attacking in the new form of warfare, and
what is needed to suppress it are just 100 men, few of them
Americans, organized in the four European squadrons.
When it comes to counterterrorist work, small *is* beautiful
because it has been proved to work. And large doesn't
work.

I have explained that the type of support the international task force will need is of the caliber available in the
67th Helicopter Squadron. The rapid response teams need
air mobility, which means helicopters in readiness on station, well-maintained and ready to go on a moment's
notice, and fixed-wing tactical troop transports for longer
flights and the silent high altitude parachute drops sometimes called for. A communications network will need to be
maintained to provide for secure, autonomous communications over the target area, using dedicated relay aircraft
or embassy stations with direct satellite links to a

"COBRA" type command group and the task force leader of the day.

Support would also come from units whose daily tasks already involve security as, for example, the U.S. Military Police responsible for guarding American military facilities in Europe, who have received specialist training by Germany's GSG9. Such specialist units contribute in a major way to a higher state of readiness without increase in manpower and cost.

To make a severe impact in the war against terrorism, we are talking about fewer than a thousand men.

MY WHOLE CAREER from my teens has been spent in different forms of warfare, both regular and irregular. I have fought or trained on five continents and have had the good fortune not only to survive man-to-man combat in the jungles and in the ruins of Beirut but to have a special glimpse into the way governments and ministries conduct their affairs. I have also seen the dark and seamy side, and just as a New York cop will experience bloody murders and drug addiction and yet go home to his wife and family, toughened and streetwise but still a civilized human being, so I believe my own experience has left me wary but has strengthened my belief that basic goodness can and will prevail, if given the proper opportunity.

That opportunity should be twofold. First, in the mind of every democracy's leader—president or prime minister —should be the will to know terrorism for what it is and how to combat it. Second, that will to win has to spread to the people to replace the fear of terrorism that presently exists.

Let me give you a homely example from my early years on a New Zealand farm. If we wanted to drive in a stake, we first had to take a sharp knife and whittle away one end until it came to a point. The point was then plunged into the previously prepared hole and hammered home with a mallet.

On that analogy, the special forces are the sharpened point, which drops into the hole prepared by intelligence. The weight of the stake pressing down on the point is the other counterterrorist forces, supported by law enforcement officers and the public. It is the president or prime minister whose weight of authority drives the stake home.

Acknowledgments

Above all, my thanks must go to Sol Stein, my publisher, for his awareness of the realities of terrorism, his continual encouragement, and his keen editorial work. George Greenfield, my friend and agent for over a decade, has also been a constant support.

The war against the terrorists goes on, but I hope that this book of mine will help shorten its duration.

Gayle Rivers
April, 1986

For Further Reading

Arab-Israeli Wars, The, Chaim Herzog. London: Arms and Armour Press Ltd., 1982; New York: Random House, 1983.
Autumn of Fury, Mohamed Heikal. London: Andre Deutsch Ltd., 1983; New York: Random House, 1983.
By Blood and Fire, Thurston Clarke. London: Hutchinson and Co. Ltd., 1981.
Fetch Felix, Lieut. Gen. Derrick Patrick. London: Hamish Hamilton Ltd., 1981; N. Pomfret, VT: David & Charles, 1981.
Libyan Sandstorm, John K. Cooley. London: Sidgwick and Jackson Ltd., 1982; New York: Holt, Rinehart & Winston, 1982.
Terrorism, Walter Laquer. London: Weidenfeld & Nicholson Ltd., 1977; Boston: Little, Brown & Co., 1979.